# *Boyd, Sweat & Beers*

## THE POSH DIARY 2008/09

Compiled by Paul Donnelly & Paul Mitchell

BOYD, SWEAT & BEERS : THE POSH DIARY 2008/09



ISBN : 978-0-9563110-0-9

First Published 2009 by
WHITE DRAGON PUBLISHING
Peterborough, England.

Cover photograph by kind permission of
David Lowndes and The Evening Telegraph

Back cover photographs by kind permission
of Paul Donnelly and David Lowndes.

Cover design by Kaye Falconer of Design Elements

# *Introduction*

All promotion sides require a mixture of skill, teamwork and good luck. I've seen four PUFC promotion winning teams and they all possessed those qualities, but the 08/09 team are different in having the added ingredients of youthful exuberance and a desire to improve themselves. Thanks for a wonderful season and now go and give those Championship boys a scare - I think 09/10 could be one hell of a season. Small we may be, but Posh we most definitely are.

*Paul Donnelly*

Thank you to everyone who has taken the time to contribute to the book, we really appreciate your efforts and enthusiasm. To the Evening Telegraph, the ever quotable Swanny and the staff at PUFC for being so supportive. Also special thanks to Chris Wilkinson for the statistical labour of love that is the excellent uptheposh.com. And, as ever, massive thanks to LondonRoad.net and PISA who can always be relied upon to be fully supportive of any scheme that promotes the greater glory of the Posh.
Finally, thank you to my girls Roma and Bella who always ask what the score is even though I know they really aren't that interested.

*Paul Mitchell*

# *Foreword*

Planning for the 08/09 season began on a beach in the Bahamas. My aim was the title and if that wasn't possible I wanted automatic promotion. I made that crystal clear to Darren, Barry and the rest of the management team. I wasn't interested in settling for the play-offs.

After a slow start the momentum began to build and the team lived up to my expectations by clinching promotion on that magnificent day at Colchester.

But we couldn't have done it without the fantastic support of our fans. They followed the team around the country in great numbers and were unstinting in their home support.

Enjoy the book and well done to all who have contributed to what is a unique record of an outstanding season.

*Darragh MacAnthony*
*Chairman*
*Peterborough United Football Club*

# *Contents*

## January

*Thank you. Boyd bless you. And Boyd bless Peterborough United Football Club.*

## February

*His team talk almost had me reaching for my kit so the players themselves must have been itching to get back out.*

## March

*You have to have bottle at this stage of the season and I believe Peterborough United are showing plenty of bottle.*

## April

*Then the manager ran forward and jumped on Joe's back and we all went completely and utterly mental.*

## May

*Glory is relative. And this season, it was relatively special down at Posh.*

## *The proceeds of this book will be donated to the following charities*

## *Free Kicks Foundation*

So then, the 08/09 season. It brought a second successive promotion, 89 points, 73 goals, dodgy penalty decisions, defeats of the big guns and international call-ups. A season that will be remembered for a fine manager creating a young, courageous team who never stopped battling. It will also be remembered by us at the Free Kicks Foundation as the season that we really found our feet as a charity and discovered an ever-expanding network of support amongst the legions of Posh fans.

Free Kicks is a small charity, based in Peterborough and dedicated to making a difference for a day to football-mad kids. Local hospitals and families nominate deserving children who are going through a tough time - we then arrange a trip to watch their favourite team in action, meet the players if possible, get photos or souvenirs. Anything to create an unforgettable day for them and their families.

We are a relatively new charity but we have achieved a lot in a short time.

There are 4 trustees of Free Kicks: Steve Thorpe - you may have seen him in the ET every day of the week - is the driving force and masterminds the fundraising and publicity side of things. Leigh Porter provides us with valuable contacts and advice. Damon Williams is a hands-on supporter of our fundraising events. That leaves me, Sam Downing, I organise the 'kicks' - our name for these days out - and liaise with the families, clubs and hospitals to make sure we are providing the best day out we can for these amazing children. I never fail to be humbled by the strength and courage that the youngsters show. While an adult facing similar problems in life would probably whine, moan and complain loudly about it these kids just get on with it and take it all in their stride. I certainly have a different outlook on life since I started working with Free Kicks.

Obviously, with Posh being our local team, it was imperative that we create a link with the club early on as we have had a steady stream of young Peterborough fans being suggested to us. Now, thanks to Leigh, Alex and Simon at the club, we have been able to provide, to date, 14 youngsters with a Posh team mascot package with nine of these happening this season alone.

These days are great as the kids get to look round London Road, say hello to the players and experience the fine aroma of Deep Heat in the dressing room. Then they get to lead the team out onto the pitch in front of thousands of cheering fans. As well as the visits to Peterborough we have arranged for another 16 'kicks' across the country, many at Posh away games, but Chelsea, Villa and Pompey have been great to us too and we hope to visit more Premiership clubs next season.

The other side of Free Kicks is the bit in the public eye, the bit that so many Posh fans have rallied round to help us with - the fundraising. Our events last season served us well enough but it has seemed that there has been a considerable swell in support from within the local community during this season, not least from the wonderful people from LondonRoad.net. As well as the events we have organised, such as the '92 in 92' Hours tour, football and cricket matches we have had donations and offers of other support from people previously only known to us by their online usernames.

Of course it helps that we have managed to build up a good relationship with the local media but we are very much aware that the hands-on help and the generosity from Posh supporters, not least from PISA, Adi Mowles, Paul Donnelly, Jack Thorpe, Mark Dowling, Andy Mills, Chris Slade, Nilesh Patel, Andy Taylor, Ian Gow and many, many more.

We would like to say a massive thank you to everybody who supports and looks out for us, everybody who has given us help in any shape or form over the last year and thanks to the mighty Posh - for making what we have achieved just that bit more enjoyable.

Here's to the 09/10 season - I have a feeling it's going to be unforgettable!

# *Smile Tickets*

The aim of Posh Smile Tickets is to raise money to purchase match day tickets at London Road which will be given to local community groups and nominated individuals. The scheme gives access to London Road to people who otherwise would not be able to experience the magic atmosphere.

All the money donated by fans to the Smile Tickets Fund will be spent at the club purchasing Match Day Tickets. This gives the club a direct benefit from the additional revenue of ticket sales. Local community groups and disadvantaged fans can apply for these Match Day Tickets, or Posh Smile Tickets, so they can enjoy watching a game of football that perhaps they would otherwise be unable to enjoy. Fans can also nominate individuals or groups for a special 'Smile Tickets Treat' as a means of acknowledging hard work, selfless acts and devotion to the community at large.

The number of tickets available for each match is limited only by the money in the Posh Smile Tickets fund.

Every pound donated is spent at the club, and in doing so some very deserving people in the local community get to enjoy a football match for free. The Smile Tickets ethos of being fan inclusive irrespective of social background or age and the club, by selling more tickets, will have more fans in the ground and the scheme enhances the club's, and the Trust's, links with the local community.

The cost of football excludes some members of our community from attending matches, but that does not make them any less Posh fans. Many of the fans who benefit from Posh Smile Tickets will be young people who will be attending their first ever match and these are the very same people who are the potential diehard fans of the future, and will be the lifeblood of the club in the years ahead.

# *Sue Ryder*

Sue Ryder Care is a charity providing compassionate care to people with end of life and long-term care needs.

Each year we provide 4 million hours of care to people with cancer, brain injury, multiple sclerosis, motor neurone disease, Huntington's and Parkinson's disease, stroke and dementia. We deliver specialist caring services in people's own homes, in the community and in our hospices and care centres enabling people to manage their treatment and live their lives to the full.

Through innovation and research we work to improve standards in long-term and end of life care. We have recently received government recognition for improving end of life care for people with long-term conditions; our research partnership with the University of Nottingam is extending skills and knowledge across the sector. We have piloted leading hospice at home services and holistic care management programmes for people with complex physical and psychological needs.

Our work goes beyond the UK. With fifty projects across 12 countries in Europe and southern Africa, Sue Ryder Care is positioned at the centre of an international health and social care partnership.

Each year we need to raise £74 million to fund our work.

# *Boyd, Sweat & Beers*

## THE POSH DIARY 2008/09

# *Pre-Season*

**30/06/08**

Pre-season training starts.

* * * * *

**06/07/08**

The full squad, with the exception of the injured Jamie Day and transfer-listed players, fly out to Marbella for an intensive training camp which will include a couple of practice matches.

* * * * *

**10/07/08**

Sergio Torres signs from Wycombe Wanderers. He follows in the footsteps of Russell Martin who joined from Wycombe earlier in the summer.

* * * * *

**12/07/08**

Peterborough United 3 - 1 Rochdale

| | |
|---|---|
| Mackail-Smith '14 | Dagnall '50 |
| Boyd '26 | |
| Potter '88 | |

**Peterborough United:** Joe Lewis (-46′), Russell Martin (-55′), Shane Blackett (-46′), Craig Morgan (-46′), Tommy Williams (-55′), George Boyd (-46′), Dean Keates, Micah Hyde (-46′), Chris Whelpdale (-46′), Craig Mackail-Smith (-46′), Aaron McLean (-46′)
Subs: James McKeown (+46′), Kieran Charnock (+46′), Chris Westwood (+46′), Alfie Potter (+46′), Billy Crook (+46′) (-75′), Liam Hatch (+46′) (-75′), Scott Rendell (+46′), Danny Andrew (+55′), Callum Reed (+55′), Darren Gourlay (+75′), Rene Howe (+75′)
**Rochdale:** Sam Russell, Simon Ramsden (-46′), Nathan Stanton, Rory McArdle (-46′), Tom Kennedy, Gary Jones (-46′), Clark Keltie (-46′), Joe Thompson (-46′), Kallum Higginbotham, Ciarán Toner, Adam le Fondre (-46′)
Subs: Nathan D'Laryea (+46′), Raphale Evans (+46′), Adam Rundle (+46′), Ben Muirhead (+46′), Chris Dagnall (+46′), Scott Wiseman (+46′)

A pre-season tournament a mere 90 minute drive away was just too good an opportunity to pass up. Posh, Rochdale, Marbella and Iran - yes, that's Iran - playing amongst the fleshpots of the Costa del Sol .

Nothing would normally get me anywhere near Marbella, especially in July, but this was too good an opportunity to miss so I bribed the wife with the promise of a good hotel and an elegant meal and we set off on Saturday afternoon. She feigned interest during the journey as I told her how lucky she was to be getting her first glimpse of the white Pele, the full-story behind Aaron McLean's transfer request, Joe Lewis' England call up and our new right back from Wycombe Wanderers; time must have flown by for her. After all, she hadn't seen Posh since our last game at Wembley so I had to make sure she knew all about the splendiferous offerings awaiting.

MPFS Marbella - hosts of the tournament - did not prove to be the easiest venue to find but after a few detours we spotted a bouncy castle, a packed car park and some football pitches so knew that we had arrived. Walking in, we were struck by both the number of green, white and red Iranian flags and the number of orange coloured blonde women in tight white clothing. Of more concern was the condition of the pitches - hard, uneven and with little grass. 'This could be dangerous,' I predicted, erroneously as it turned out.

At the bar, with 20 minutes until the kick off, we found two Rochdale fans but no other Poshies. Then we found out why we had seen nothing of the Peterborough contingent. Rochdale had taken one look at the pitches and said, "We're not playing on there", and Iran had had a bust up with Charlton - who they were meant to be playing the following Tuesday - and pulled out of the tournament in a political tantrum without telling their supporters. Posh, we were told, were now playing Rochdale in a 90 minute friendly back at their La Cala training resort twenty five minutes away.

The chase along the main road was quite exciting, as was the language about 'typical bloody Boro organisation', and followed by the Rochdale fans we eventually reached the lush, plush 'new' venue. Conveniently just 5 minutes away from the hotel we'd left our bags in an hour before.

Well, because of the cock-up, we missed the first 15 minutes. That included, I was informed by the posh.com press boys (so it might not be correct), a McKail-Smith headed goal from a Whelpdale cross. After about 25 minutes, however, George Boyd made all the rushing around worthwhile when he scored a peach of a goal that just summed up what he is all about - class and magic. Posh controlled the first half comfortably . The new lad, Russell Martin, looked very composed on the ball and, my wife said, very fit. McLean was running himself into the ground, which was good to see because there had been concerns about how he would react to not being a Wolves player. Fergie gave Tommy Williams grief for giving away too many free kicks and Joe Lewis still looked like he needed a good meal.

The two Rochdale fans we'd adopted were claiming that they were obviously putting their best team on in the second half because they didn't recognise any of the players. This turned out to be because they thought Rochdale were the team in blue and not the ones playing in their second strip. Very embarrassed they were.

Lots of changes in the second half saw a clumsy Charnock challenge give away a soft penalty - you'll read that phrase again in a few pages. Charlie Lee got clobbered and was carried off as the tackles got a little tasty and the Spanish ref completely lost control for a few minutes. McKeown made some good stops, Westwood looked off the pace as he'd only just started training and Rendell, Hatch and Howe all looked as good as the Rochdale strikers but not as good as our first half pair.

The real star, though, was Alfie Potter, who tantalised and teased the defenders as he ran amok, scoring a lovely curled goal just before the end to make the final score 3 - 1 to Posh. "He's going to put Whelps under real pressure this year," I said. I'm glad I don't gamble.

*Greg Bedford*

* * * * *

**16/07/08**

Craig Morgan is named as captain for the forthcoming season.

* * * * *

**17/07/08**

## Peterborough Utd XI 0 - 2 Fisher Athletic

Top secret friendly played behind closed-doors. It might not have even taken place. Posh lost, allegedly, but we couldn't find anyone to talk 'on the record' about it.

* * * * *

**18/07/08**

Aaron McLean is taken off the transfer list at his own request. The allure of the Black Country seems to have worn off.

* * * * *

**19/07/08**

## Peterborough United 4 - 1 Liverpool XI

| Peterborough United | Liverpool XI |
|---|---|
| McLean 40 | Bruna 60 |
| Potter 45 | |
| Lee 73 | |
| Rendell 87 | |

Att: 2,295.

**Peterborough United:** Joe Lewis (-46'), Craig Morgan (-88'), Chris Westwood (-60'), Micah Hyde (-60'), Aaron McLean(-60'), George Boyd, Craig Mackail-Smith, Chris Whelpdale (-88'), Alfie Potter, Tommy Williams (-60'), Paul Coutts (-60')

Subs: Shane Blackett (+60′), Charlie Lee (+60′), Scott Rendell (+60′), Dean Keates (+60′), James McKeown (+46′), Kieran Charnock (+60′), Callum Reed (+88′), Darren Gourlay (+88′)
**Liverpool XI:** Chris Oldfield (-46′), Martin Kelly, Gary MacKay-Steven, Kelemen Dávid (-46′), Godwin Antwi, Steven Irwin, Ryan Crowther (-46′), Ryan Flynn, Craig Lindfield, Nathan Eccleston (-46′), Gerardo Bruna (-68′)
Subs: Ronald Huth (+46′), Hakan Duyan (+46′), Ódé Norbert, Pölöskei Zsolt (+46′), Alexander Kacaniklic (+68′), Jordy Brouwer (+46′)

My last Liverpool match was over 15 years ago, stood on the Kop, hungover and skint after being fleeced by the Scouse tout (great sense of humour though), watching Englands once-finest play Blackburn off the park.

Fast forward to July 2008, Saturday, pre-season, the mighty Liverpool are in town, it was too good to miss. Unfortunately Liverpool were in a lot of towns that pre-season day, I think Posh were 8th or 9th on the list. It just didn't seem right seeing players that young in the famous kit, most of them made Alfie Potter look old. Ah, Alfie, he carried on where he left off in the FA Cup and tortured the Liverpool defence to the point that I swear one of them was crying.

A legend was also born in front of that small crowd in July, with the appearance of triallist Paul Coutts. A couple of assured touches, good holding play, sign him up (we did). 4-1 win, a good day out and my son and his mate came away happy, what more can you ask for?

*Trev's Mate*

* * * * *

**22/07/08**

## Stevenage Borough 0 - 2 Peterborough United

McLean '39
Rendell '43

**Stevenage Borough:** James Russell (-46'), Eddie Anaclet, Ronnie Henry (-38'), Mark Albrighton, Scott Laird, Mitchell Cole (-75'), Michael Bostwick (-66'), Gary Mills (-46'), Daryl McMahon, Anthony Thomas (-44'), Lee Boylan (-66')
Subs: Michael Jordan (+46'), Luke Oliver (+38'), David Bridges (+75'), Laurie Wilson (+66'), Andy Drury (+46'), Iyseden Christie (+44'), Craig Westcarr (+66')
**Peterborough United:** James McKeown, Chris Westwood, Kieran Charnock, Tommy Williams, Paul Coutts (-61'), Shaun Batt, George Boyd (-61'), Charlie Lee, Callum Reed (-46'), Scott Rendell, Aaron McLean (-46')
Subs: Micah Hyde (+61'), Alfie Potter (+61'), Dean Keates (+46'), Craig Mackail-Smith (+46')

It was on a warm July evening that we cruised down the A1 to watch a pre-season friendly at Broadhall Way. I'd love to write an amusing and exciting account of this match but, unfortunately, it was bloody damn boring. In fact it was quite possibly the most stereotypical friendly I've ever seen.

Posh cantered to an easy 2-0 victory courtesy of goal machine Aaron McLean and Cambridge's finest, Scott Rendell (for the record it was most certainly a tap in). It also saw the relatively unknown Paul Coutts make an impressive start in a Posh shirt.

One would assume that George Boyd would be the star of the show considering he was returning to his old stomping ground, and though he did receive rapturous applause and a standing ovation from all 48 fans in attendance, it was the lamppost on trial from Fisher

Athletic that caught my attention; yes, that's right, a certain Shaun Batt.

When I saw Batt warming up I turned to my mate and said: "When the hell did Michael Jordan start playing for us?" Having said that, this ridiculously tall lad had some talent, in a kind of amusing way. At times his legs looked like they didn't belong to the rest of his body and an image of a headless chicken came to mind. But when he got going he was like a rocket, happily playing on both wings and scaring both full-backs alike From that moment on, I knew he was going to become a London Road cult hero.

Also, I'd like it put on record, it was at this game, and this game only, that I finally got the "I've seen Micah Hyde shoot" T-shirt. Result.

Following a couple of sherbets in the friendly clubhouse and a cheeky Pizza Hut across the way it was off home to Peterborough, with the thought that perhaps, just perhaps, there could be an interesting season ahead.

*Matthew Barber*

* * * * *

**23/07/08**

## Cefn Druids 2 - 2 Peterborough United

| | |
|---|---|
| Feeney | Jirbandey |
| Hussaney | Lyons |

Not at work today so think I will have a lie in before having a day gardening and walking the dogs. The sun is cracking the flags as for a change we are experiencing a lovely summer's day. I need a relaxing day as still tired from the trip back from Stevenage. Go on the internet to see what is happening in the world and I notice through google that Posh are playing at Cefn Mawr this evening. Who and where are they?

Nothing on the Posh website, phone the club - no reply. Phone Cefn Mawr - no reply. Phone the lads I go to games with but they are all at work and know nothing about it. Check out where Cefn Mawr is and find it is not far from Wrexham and think: sod the gardening a trip to North Wales sounds a far better idea - even on my own. I phone the wife and in the afternoon set off not knowing if there's really a game or not.

Arrived at the ground after venturing down a dusty track and found someone in the ground who told me, "Fergie said he would send a team and we kick off at 6.30pm". It was their manager Wayne Phillips who told me that he played with Fergie at Wrexham. I was made very welcome as he made me a cuppa and admitted he didn't expect any visiting supporters tonight. A minibus rolled up and some Posh Juniors and Dave Oldfield got out looking really cramped after their journey. Adam Smith and Josh Low then turned up by car. I was treated royally by Dave Oldfield who was shocked someone had travelled to the game and I had a good natter with some of the Posh youngsters (who are a real friendly bunch). I had a couple of drinks in their clubhouse which was superb and then watched the game with about 150 local fans.

The game was entertaining with Smith and Low looking head and shoulders above everyone else. Cefn Druids who are the oldest football club in Wales were well up for the game and treated the match as though they were playing the Posh first team. The game ended up at 2-2 with the players giving their all in about 80 degrees. The youngsters who stood out were Scott Ginty and Josh Jirbandey.

A match day programme was issued by Cefn Druids, the line up showing Posh first team. I was given a team sheet by the club secretary which showed the true teams. The Posh team (including subs) was: Sam Cole, Aled Austin, Danny Andrews, Billy Crook, Darren Gorlay, Josh Jirbandey, Josh Low, Lewis Webb, Scott Ginty, Craig Carver, Adam Smith, Jack Lyons, Nathan Korenteng, Charlie Dove, Luke Abrahams, Carl Piergianni.

All in all a good day out: thoroughly enjoyed a trip to a new ground, was made very welcome by everyone especially the Posh players. Only grumble is that Posh didn't advertise this game and it was sheer luck that I found out about it. No other Posh fans were there which was a shame as I am sure others would have made the trip if the game had been advertised.

*Clive Taylor*

* * * * *

**26/07/08**

## Rushden & Diamonds 2 -1 Peterborough Utd

Challinor '44 Keates '53
McDonald '69

Att: 941

**Rushden and Diamonds:** Alan Marriott, Curtis Osano, Gareth Jelleyman, Chris Hope, Jon Challinor (-64'), Lee Phillips (-60'), Daryl Clare (-60'), Scott Mitchell (-89'), Lee Tomlin, Sagi Burton, Marcus Kelly
Subs: Phil Gulliver (+89'), Dean McDonald (+60'), Michael Rankine (+60'), Michael Corcoran (+64'), Justyn Roberts

**Peterborough United:** Joe Lewis, Russell Martin, Craig Morgan, Chris Westwood (-57'), Micah Hyde, Aaron McLean, George Boyd, Dean Keates, Craig Mackail-Smith (-76'), Chris Whelpdale (-57'), Tommy Williams (-57')
Subs: Charlie Lee (+57'), Scott Rendell (+76'), Kieran Charnock (+57'), Alfie Potter, Danny Andrew (+57')

I don't normally go to friendlies. Players not giving a stuff, managers wanting to give everyone a game and fans generally disinterested. In fact, I'd usually not even cross the road to go to a friendly but I'm about to prove that wrong.

Rushden's ground is about a mile from my house and I've told a friend that I will be there (must have been a bit tipsy at the time). I won a signed Posh football in a raffle and he's going to give it to me at the game. Weighing up all the options, I decide to go on my pushbike.

Arriving at the ground with my wife I discover very few people arrive at football grounds by bicycle. In fact we appeared to be the only ones, certainly from the away support. We lock them together precariously next to the fire exit and pay our money to get in. Not really expecting a huge crowd for the game but a reasonable turn out from Posh of about 150.

Now for the game: a 'massive' Cup Final between the best team in Northamptonshire and the best (by far) team in Cambridgeshire – the Maunsell Cup Final. This will be the first chance I get to see the future Posh captain Russ Martin. The right back slot has been pretty vacant over the last few years so it would be nice to see some quality there for a change. Also good to see a couple of ex-Posh players lining up for Diamonds - Gareth Jelleyman and captain Sagi Burton.

The first half was fairly even with Posh carving out a few half chances but not really troubling the opposition goalkeeper. Rushden had a goal (rightly) disallowed for offside but manage to go a goal up in stoppage time after a howler by Tom Williams who I assume was sunbathing rather than concentrating.

Second half Posh started brightly and equalised on 53 minutes with an excellent free kick by Dean 'Hobbit' Keates. Now one of the main reasons I never go to friendly games makes itself apparent – substitutions. Ten minutes after we bring on three subs Rushden score. If we are pointing fingers of blame - and why not - then Morgan should've been a lot stronger on the edge of the box and not allow their sub to score. We make another sub, Rendall on for CMS, to try and claw back the coveted trophy but to no avail.

Not wanting to see Rushden lift the trophy we make a quick exit to find both bikes still there! Let's hope we play better this season or it could turn into a very long year.

*Andy Mills*

* * * * *

**28/07/08**

The Day of the Pen. Aaron McLean signs a new four-year contract. Shaun Batt pens one-year deal and Paul Coutts agrees three-year contract. Charlie Lee agrees new four-year contract at London Road. The faithful are dancing in the streets of PE1.

* * * * *

**29/07/08**

## Peterborough United 0 - 2 West Ham United

Bellamy '3
Bellamy '42

Att:5,352

**Peterborough United:** Joe Lewis, Russell Martin, Shane Blackett (-61′), Craig Morgan (-73′), Charlie Lee (-67′), Aaron McLean (-61′), George Boyd (-73′), Dean Keates (-61′), Craig Mackail-Smith, Chris Whelpdale (-61′), Tommy Williams
Subs: Chris Westwood (+61′), Scott Rendell (+61′), Micah Hyde (+67′), James McKeown, Kieran Charnock (+73′), Alfie Potter (+73′), Paul Coutts (+61′), Shaun Batt (+61′)
**West Ham United:** Robert Green (-73′), Lucas Neill, Anton Ferdinand (-88′), Matthew Upson, Valon Behrami (-67′), Scott Parker, Julien Faubert, Craig Bellamy Goal Goal (-73′), Kyle Reid (-83′), Carlton Cole, Mark Noble
Subs: Joe Widdowson (+67′), Calum Davenport, Marek Št?ch (+73′), Tony Stokes, Jack Collison (+88′), Hayden Mullins, Freddie Sears (+73′), Junior Stanislas (+83′)

I had decided not to attend any pre-season friendlies as the previous years offerings were about as enjoyable as a diving lesson without breathing apparatus in one of those new lakes that had appeared in the car park adjacent to Colin Hill's excuse for a football stadium.

However as the day wore on I became more and more frustrated with a client who seemed to enjoy breaking down in tears every hour whilst I installed a new kitchen in her house. I had to deal with complaints ranging from "your fitters keep passing wind and swearing when I'm out of the kitchen" to "some of these new floor tiles are 1mm higher than others", "are you insured if I trip over and smash my face on the new worktops" to this, and it's a corker: "the water out of the hot tap is too hot!"

I needed a beer and a footy match where I could stand on the terraces and redirect Mrs Harris' menopausal tension through the medium of Craig Bellamy and West Ham. Met up with Mowlsey in Charters at 5.30 and 6 pints of Milly's Maggots ABV 6.2% later I was ready for one of Jolly Jack's burgers. Then through the turnstiles that each season seem to shrink, up the 'tunnel of love' and another season of hopes and dreams is about to begin.

After two mins and 49 seconds Craig Bellamy collected the ball: "You're f****** useless Bellamy" I yelled out, three secs later he'd scored. 1-0 West Ham.

The robust Green was in no mood to let Posh into the game, as he made a one-handed save to deny an acrobatic shot by Aaron McLean and a finger-tip save to deny Craig Mackail-Smith on the half-hour mark. Posh captain Craig Morgan then had near chances before West Ham United went further ahead. The goal came in the 42nd minute in a move started at the back by Neill who sent over a good ball which was met perfectly by the f****** useless Bellamy. 2-0 West Ham

Second half saw some changes and the first opportunity to see some of the 'new kids on the block'. The lad from Scotland, Paul Coutts, looks a real find, have no idea where we got him from but he was so confident on the ball. Indeed he didn't waste a pass and could be a real asset this season if he develops.

Posh came within an inch of grabbing something, only for George Boyd's shot to hit the post and come bouncing back out. It proved to be another good work-out for Ferguson's men and one that gave me considerable encouragement for the forthcoming season, back to

Charters for another beer, daughter drove me home and off with my coat.

"Any phone calls pet?"

"Yeah. Mrs Harris wants you to ring her back."

"What's up with her?

"She used her hob for the first time tonight and burnt her sausages, she wants to know what you're going to do about it"

"Buy her some f*****g mustard!"

*Paul Donnelly*

* * * * *

**02/08/08**

## Corby Town 2 - 2 Peterborough United XI

| Corby Town | Peterborough United XI |
|---|---|
| Deehan '34 (pen) | Crow '32 (pen.) |
| Stevenson '79 | Low '63 |

Att: 308

**Corby Town:** Mark Osborne, Dean West, Adam Jones, Mark Warren, Leon Hibbert, Matt O'Halloran, Steve Towers, Matt Nolan, Deehan, Oliver Burgess,Jon Stevenson

**Peterborough United:** Mark Tyler, Callum Reed (-39'), Jamie Day (-60'), Sam Gaughran, Shane Blackett, Sergio Torres (-46'), Billy Crook (-78'), Adam Smith, Josh Low (-74'), Danny Crow (-69'), Liam Hatch (-85')
Subs: Josh Jirbandey (+39'), Sam Cole, Danny Andrew (+60'), Lewis Webb (+46'), Luke Abraham (+74'), Scott Ginty (+78'), Nathan Koranteng (+69'), Jack Lyons (+85')

This will be the first friendly I have ever attended as I was pestered into going by my 10 year old daughter who is now a Posh fanatic.

We set off early so I could meet up with Clive from Bradford. Sat nav set and away we go but could we find the ground, could we hell. A quick call to Clive guides us to the ground and we get there with 10 mins to spare. At the gate a nice little gate man asks for £10 for a disabled supporter - I nearly fell out my chair and asked if he was taking the piss. He wouldn't haggle so under sufference we paid and entered the tin pot ground.

Some flag waving from the usual suspects greets kick off with Tyler the legend in goal and Crow up front. After a dull 20 odd mins we get a penalty which is converted by Crow but Corby immediately hit back with a penalty of their own.

There is a sudden burst of action from the stewards as a flare is let off - are we in Corby or at the San Siro? The second-half starts in the same boring style until Joshua Low bags a quality finish. Yet again Corby find the net for a 2-2 draw. The highlight of the day was the flare but who threw it? Answers on a postcard please.

*Paul Richardson*

* * * * *

**04/08/08**

## Peterborough United 0 - 2 Manchester United

Martin '39 (o.g.)
Gibson '68

Att: 13,042

**Peterborough United:** Joe Lewis (-46'), Russell Martin (-46'), Shane Blackett (-57'), Craig Morgan, Chris Westwood (-46'), Scott Rendell (-46'), Micah Hyde (-46'), Aaron McLean (-46'), Paul Coutts (-46'), Chris Whelpdale (-75'), Sergio Torres (-46')
Subs: Charlie Lee (+46'), George Boyd (+46'), Dean Keates (+46'), Craig Mackail-Smith (+46'), James McKeown, Liam Hatch (+46'), Jamie Day

(+57′), Kieran Charnock (+46′), Tommy Williams (+75′), Shaun Batt (+46′), Mark Tyler (+46′)
**Manchester United:** Tomasz Kuszczak (-67′), John O'Shea, Patrice Evra (-46′), Rio Ferdinand (-46′), Wes Brown (-46′), Darren Fletcher (-67′), Fraizer Campbell (-46′), Carlos Tévez (-46′), David Gray, Nani (-58′), Rafael da Silva
Subs: Jonny Evans (+46′), Darron Gibson (+67′), Lee Martin (+46′), Craig Cathcart (+46′), Ron-Robert Zieler (+67′), Tom Cleverley (+46′), Fabio da Silva (+46′), Possebon (+58′)

Nothing. No match report or even the offer of one. I think Man United won and the Director of Football had his photo taken giving the thumbs-up whilst standing next to Sir Alex Ferguson.

# *August*

**09/08/08**

## Southend United 1 - 0 Peterborough United

Clarke '76

Att: 8,665 (1,468 away).

**Southend United:** Steve Mildenhall, Simon Francis, Nicky Bailey, Peter Clarke, Adam Barrett, Lee Barnard, James Walker (-83'), Damian Scannell (-71'), Franck Moussa, Dan Harding, Paul Furlong (-88')
Subs: Anthony Grant (+83'), Alex Revell (+88'), Osei Sankofa, Kevin Betsy (+71'), Ian Joyce
**Peterborough United:** Joe Lewis, Russell Martin, Craig Morgan, Chris Westwood, Charlie Lee, Aaron McLean, George Boyd, Dean Keates, Craig Mackail-Smith, Chris Whelpdale (-80'), Tommy Williams
Subs: Shane Blackett, Scott Rendell, Micah Hyde, Sergio Torres (+80'), Mark Tyler

Hopes were high as Posh began the season with a trip to sunny Southend-on-Sea. My son, Craig, had elected to drive and after picking up Mowlsey and Nilesh we left Peterborough in bright sunshine around 8am. We arrived at the seaside with our buckets and spades and after parking the car on the promenade we made our way to the designated watering hole and, beer in hand, claimed a table outside.

The only thing of interest in the next couple of hours (other than who was getting the next round in) was a very attractive young lady who had just bought a parking ticket. Whilst in the process of taking her baby out of the car a gust of wind had blown the ticket into oncoming traffic. After strapping the baby into the pushchair she realised she couldn't find her ticket, and obviously hadn't got a clue were it had gone. Craig sprang to the rescue and stopped the traffic whilst he retrieved the errant ticket. A chorus of cheers went up as Craig received her grateful thanks. I do believe if she had not had the baby he would have missed the game and taken a stroll down the beach with her.

After Nilesh gracefully declined another pint and revealed he had now achieved his life-long ambition of matching Mowlsey and I, drink for drink for a period of two hours, we moved on to a chippy. Having now soaked up most of the beer we parked near to the ground and looked to continue the 'start of season celebrations'. We finally found a pub where the window-lickers had taken up residence and our last couple of pints were consumed amongst our friends from Forever Posh, or whatever it is they call themselves now.

The game was far from the spectacle we had expected and despite Posh controlling the game for long periods (especially during the first half) we were unable to break down the excellent defence of our opponents, and a draw looked the likely outcome. Unfortunately Southend had a good 15 min spell and it was in that period that they scored what was to be the decisive goal. We resumed total control of the ball after that but, other than a header from McLean which went wide of the post - he should've done better - we couldn't break them down.

So our introduction back into Division One had ended up a losing one, but by the time we arrived back home we had all agreed that it was just a blip and the season was still going to be one of high expectation and hope and not a fight against relegation.

*Barry Matthews*

* * * * *

**12/08/08**

League Cup

Bristol City 2 - 1 Peterborough United

Carey '53 Boyd '17

Brooker '85

Att: 5,684 (171 away).

**Bristol City:** Chris Weale, Jamie McAllister, Liam Fontaine, Louis Carey, Steve Brooker, Nicky Maynard (-87'), Michael McIndoe, Cole Skuse, Ivan Sproule (-62'), Christian Ribeiro (-34'), Lee Johnson
Subs: Bradley Orr, Jamie McCombe, David Noble, Brian Wilson (+34'), Gavin Williams (+62'), Lee Trundle (+87'), Stephen Henderson
**Peterborough United:** Joe Lewis, Russell Martin, Craig Morgan, Chris Westwood, Charlie Lee, Aaron McLean (-73'), George Boyd, Dean Keates, Craig Mackail-Smith, Tommy Williams, Sergio Torres (-87')
Subs: Shane Blackett, Scott Rendell (+73'), Micah Hyde, Liam Hatch (+87'), Paul Coutts, Shaun Batt, Mark Tyler

Great draw in the crappy league cup, thanks whoever did that.

There was no way I was going to go but after a bit of persuasion from Nilesh and Ant I said I would if I could get a full car, which is seven. They only went and sorted it didn't they.

Anyway off we jolly well went, made great time and found a pub only a few miles away from the ground. After a bite to eat and a few pints (not for me of course) we found a parking space at the back of a car dealership, walked through some of the biggest puddles I have seen and entered Ashton Gate, a ground I have always liked as it's a proper ground with a good atmosphere.

We totally murdered them all game, scored at a good time but just couldn't get the second to put the game to bed. The locals gave Posh a great reception at the end of the game knowing full well they had got away with it and we left happy in defeat which is a rare occurrence.

As we left the ground a few kids who thought they were hard had a few words. Being an old man nowadays I let it go until, that is, I saw them walking along the road later and, speeding up to thirty miles an hour, I drove through a particularly large puddle and gave them probably the first wash they'd ever had.

If we end up playing them next season I hope they don't hold a grudge.

*Adi Mowles*

* * * * *

**16/08/08**

## Peterborough United 3 - 0 Leyton Orient

Mackail-Smith '44
McLean '50
Mackail-Smith '69

Att: 6,643 (898 away).

**Peterborough United:** Joe Lewis, Russell Martin, Shane Blackett (-81′), Craig Morgan, Chris Westwood, Charlie Lee (-78′), McLean, George Boyd, Dean Keates, Craig Mackail-Smith, Sergio Torres (-81′)
Subs: Scott Rendell, Micah Hyde (+78′), Chris Whelpdale (+81′), Tommy Williams (+81′), Mark Tyler
**Leyton Orient:** Glenn Morris, Stephen Purches, Danny Granville (-51′), Tamika Mkandawire, Brian Saah, John Melligan (-64′), Adam Chambers, Wayne Gray (-71′), Sean Thornton, Adam Boyd, Jason Demetriou
Subs: Alton Thelwell, Simon Dawkins (+71′), Paul Terry, Aiden Palmer (+51′), Ryan Jarvis (+64′)

Majestic. Imposing. Brilliant. Excellent. Magical. A joy to watch – the posh.netters just can't come up with enough superlatives to describe Posh's second half performance against a hapless Leyton Orient at London Road. Torres started on the right wing, with Blackett coming in at left back – and on the back of this performance, they'll stay there.

The real star performers, however, were the holy trinity of CMS, McLean and Boyd. Mackail-Smith just never stopped running and was a constant threat to the Os defenders, who looked terrified every time he got anywhere near the ball – and rightly so, as he scored twice. McLean collected his League Two Golden Boot trophy before the match and then opened his account for this season with a fine strike.

George Boyd, meanwhile, was just different gravy. The talismanic left winger tormented the entire Orient side and had everyone in the ground applauding his sheer brilliance. The boy, as they say, is a bit special. He's our Matt Le Tissier, and if he keeps this form up, Darragh may soon get a chance to enjoy his pre-season ambition of turning down a bid of £4m for one of his players.

Next Saturday, we're at Scunthorpe, who are still looking to earn their first points of the season. Looks like they'll have to wait a little longer.

*Jack Thorpe*

* * * * *

**23/08/08**

## Scunthorpe United 1 - 0 Peterborough United

Hayes '44 (pen.)

Att: 4,717 (802 away).

**Scunthorpe United:** Joe Murphy, Marcus Williams, Izzy Iriekpen, Cliff Byrne, Garry Thompson, Paul Hayes (-83'), Gary Hooper (-87'), Grant McCann, Sam Togwell, Kevan Hurst (-76'), Krystian Pearce
Subs: Martyn Woolford (+87'), Jonathan Forte (+83'), Josh Lillis, Andrew Wright, Ian Morris (+76')
**Peterborough United:** Joe Lewis, Russell Martin, Shane Blackett, Charlie Lee, Aaron McLean, George Boyd, Dean Keates, Craig Mackail-Smith, Jamie Day (-71'), Kieran Charnock (-60'), Sergio Torres (-81')
Subs: Liam Hatch (+81'), Chris Whelpdale (+60'), Tommy Williams (+71'), Shaun Batt, Mark Tyler

I planned to do as many away days as possible at the start of the season, so I wasn't going to turn down what I thought would be a relatively easy trip to Scunthorpe. I was Doncaster bound by 10am and didn't have to spend much time there as the trains to Scunthorpe were reasonably frequent.

At Donny I mixed in with a friendly bunch of our fans that'd jumped off trains from just about everywhere. I ended up standing all the way into Scunthorpe which didn't go down well with my legs. Then came the most depressing part of the journey. As you go into Scunthorpe by train you pass the ground and get a good look of where you will be spending the afternoon. However, after you've admired the ground your train keeps going, and going, and going until coming to a halt another 10 minutes down the line. Upon leaving the train just about every Posh fan wandered past the large rotting unmarked Double Decker bus that sat outside (remember that bus) and into a nice little pub around the corner.

After leaving the pub a few friendly locals pointed me towards the ground which was practically downhill all the way. I made it a lot quicker than first estimated and had time for another beer with a couple of friends. We took our seats inside the ground and as ever with our fans, there was confusion over seating as people had pre-paid tickets and many had paid on the gate, thus not having an allocated seat. Everyone took a seat hoping for our first away win of the season. Everyone was in good spirits but the Posh chances failed to materialise and Scunthorpe looked the stronger side.

The football was end to end and reasonably entertaining but no one was performing in the final third of the pitch. Then came the breakthrough none of the travelling 1000 odd wanted to see, Kieran Charnock clattering into an advancing Scunthorpe player who went down like a sack of spuds, which resulted in a penalty. I stood complaining that it may have been out of the area, but no one seemed to agree. So I sat back down and watched them slot home the penalty. The game was drawing to a close and we were all sat with glum faces watching Posh try pretty hard to get an equaliser but we just couldn't find the net.

Just when we thought it couldn't get any worse a tannoy announcement informed us that: "All Peterborough fans going home by train will have to be bussed back to the station in Doncaster as there is a problem on the line between here and your destination." Leaving the ground the local constabulary directed us to the old beat up bus from the station ready to take us to Doncaster.

We all sat around discussing the game, the journey, and what time we were going to get home and twigged that this bus malarkey was working in our favour as we'd get back to Doncaster before the train we were due to catch from Scunthorpe, allowing us to get an earlier connection home. The best bit of the day. We boarded a busy train back to Peterborough and again I stood the whole way. I got back to Stamford by 8pm and despite the result and events thought to myself: 'what a fun day.'

*Glen Townsend.*

* * * * *

**27/08/08**

Dominic Green signs from Dagenham and Redbridge for an undisclosed fee. He joins Posh in preference to two Championship clubs and League One rivals Huddersfield Town.

Adam Smith has his contract cancelled by mutual consent.

Liam Hatch signs for Darlington on three-month loan deal.

* * * * *

**29/09/08**

Josh Low joins Cheltenham Town after his contract is terminated by mutual consent.
Centre back Kieran Charnock is placed on the transfer list. Giving away a penalty with a challenge that Hong Kong Phooey would've been proud of doesn't appear to have impressed the boss.

* * * * *

**30/08/08**

Peterborough United 1 - 2 Hartlepool United

Boyd '78 — Monkhouse '58, Barker '59

Att: 5,728 (391 away).

**Peterborough United:** Joe Lewis, Russell Martin, Shane Blackett, Craig Morgan, Micah Hyde (-69'), Aaron McLean, George Boyd, Dean Keates (-69'), Craig Mackail-Smith, Jamie Day, Sergio Torres
Subs: Charlie Lee (+69'), Scott Rendell, Chris Whelpdale (+69'), Dominic Green, Mark Tyler
**Hartlepool United:** Arran Lee-Barratt, Jamie McCunnie, Ritchie Humphreys, Michael Nelson, Sam Collins, Gary Liddle, Ritchie Jones, Joel Porter (-75'), Andy Monkhouse (-84'), James Brown (-59'), Antony Sweeney
Subs: Richard Barker (+59'), Alan Power, David Foley (+75'), Matty Robson (+84'), Jonny Rowell

Everybody can remember their first time. Mine was with an older wo... Hang on, sorry, wrong first time. Mine was a friendly against Ipswich Town in the early 80s. I can't recall a lot – my dad and I sat in the Main Stand and I recall it being dark and cavernous; Alan Brazil, I think, scored and Ipswich wore orange.

The Hartlepool game was on the weekend after my birthday (33 if anyone's counting) and my eldest daughter Maisie decided that it would be an ideal present if she 'took' me to the match. She had been to the Steve Cooper memorial match a few years before, but this, at the age of six, was to be her first proper game.

We set off mid-morning so that we could arrive in Peterborough at a decent time. The journey down was passed trying to teach her the few songs that don't have swear words in and trying to explain to her how a 33 year old man can love a 23 year old man and mummy at the same time. She agreed that she too would love George Boyd.

We parked up at Bishop's Road and walked to Rivergate to meet my sister for lunch. I had left it to Maisie to choose and we went to the little Italian for a pizza and a bit of a catch up. Aside from a stack of beer with your mates, there is no finer way to build up to a match. We turned back to Woolies for some dods before heading for the ground. I will admit to looking on a little enviously at those sprawled out in the beer garden of Charters.

For the first time in my life I walked around the Main Stand, past the dribs and drabs of Pool fans and entered the Glebe from the Moy's End through the family turnstile. I was pleased to see that Maisie was admitted for free. Well done Posh.

Weather wise, 2008 wasn't a vintage summer by any stretch of the imagination, but this particular day was sweltering and I can't remember ever having watched a game in hotter conditions. On the very back row of the upper tier (where Maisie had wanted to sit) the air was listless. Fortunately there were not many people around us so we could spread out and get as comfortable as possible to try to cool down. We failed.

Maisie isn't really a footballing kind of girl, she'll sit and watch it with me on the telly but soon gets bored. This afternoon though, she kept up a constant stream of questions, even if they were mostly about if anyone was winning yet, which one was George Boyd and what was going on. I felt as though I was imparting great wisdom, although the truth may be a little different from that.

The match was poor. Posh dominated possession and had the majority of chances without really looking dangerous. Hartlepool had three chances and scored twice. The crowd was about 6,000 and I doubt many remember the game (I'd forgotten most of it by the time we'd got home). It was that kind of afternoon, although there may be a couple of Hartlepool fans on their first away day who will remember this game for ever – they made a bit of noise and looked like they'd had a good time and Joe Lewis is probably still haunted by a shocking afternoon – although his decision making was no worse than mine when I chose not to put shorts on.

Most important to me though is that I think we had enough fun so that my beautiful daughter Maisie will remember the day for ever. Part of me hopes so – I would be very proud to keep going with her, but part of me really worries what I might have inflicted on her.

*Stuart Lee*

* * * * *

**31/08/08**

| | | P | W | D | L | Pts |
|---|---|---|---|---|---|---|
| 1 | Leicester | 4 | 3 | 1 | 0 | 10 |
| 2 | Oldham | 4 | 3 | 1 | 0 | 10 |
| | | | | | | |
| 20 | Posh | 4 | 1 | 0 | 3 | 3 |

# *September*

**01/09/08**

Goalkeeper Shwan Jalal moves to Bournemouth on a two-year deal.

Danny Crow, the sloth-in-the-box, has his contract cancelled by mutual consent.

Fulham defender Gabriel Zakuani joins on a one-month loan deal.

* * * * *

**06/09/08**

## Peterborough United 5 - 4 Bristol Rovers

| | |
|---|---|
| Mackail-Smith '16 | Elliott '30 |
| McLean '23 | Blackett '54 (o.g.) |
| Mackail-Smith '51 (pen) | Hughes '74 |
| Mackail-Smith '65 | Lambert '85 |
| Rendell '83 | |

Att: 4,876 (301 away).

**Peterborough United:** Joe Lewis, Russell Martin, Shane Blackett, Chris Westwood, Charlie Lee (-82'), Aaron McLean (-39'), George Boyd, Dean Keates, Craig Mackail-Smith, Jamie Day, Sergio Torres (-55')
Subs: Scott Rendell (+39'), Paul Coutts (+82'), Chris Whelpdale (+55'), Tommy Williams, Mark Tyler

**Bristol Rovers:** Steve Phillips, Chris Lines (-82'), Steve Elliott, Stuart Campbell, Rickie Lambert, Darryl Duffy (-67'), Jeff Hughes, David Pipe, Byron Anthony, Craig Disley, Aaron Lescott
Subs: Ryan Green, Craig Hinton, Mike Green, Jo Kuffour (+67'), Ben Hunt (+82')

Along came September with Posh having tasted victory only once. The arrival of Bristol Rovers with the in-form Rickie Lambert meant that securing three points was going to be tough and nearly all of the 4,500 Posh fans would have taken at least a battling point or a scrappy win. The TV cameras were down and London Road prepared itself for a midday kick-off. They say football is a 'funny old game', and the adage was never truer that afternoon.

Having been in the press box for all of Posh's games so far, I took the opportunity to re-unite myself with the London Road terrace, and more importantly slink down to Ebs to treat myself to a pre-match beer…or four. Now firstly, there is something about a lunchtime kick-off that is against the norm; one of those is watching Soccer AM in the pub, an inherently wrong experience, and secondly it's usually not a patch on the games that stick to the traditional kick-off times. How wrong could I have been? The crowds at Posh had been getting bigger in recent times but the presence of Sky television meant there was hardly a soul on the surrounding roads, and the space on the terrace was plentiful.

Rovers started the better but the wonderful CMS gave Posh the lead after outpacing their back-line and slotting past the keeper. Ten minutes later, Mackail-Smith created an opportunity for his strike partner, McLean, who squeezed past the defence to make it 2-0. It was very comfortable for Posh as they looked to coast their way to the three points. However, the game was turned on its head as Bristol Rovers defender and one-time Posh target Steven Elliott made it 2-1 from a fairly innocuous free-kick, and moments later McLean fell awkwardly after a challenge and was stretchered off with a suspected dislocated shoulder. Half time came and went with no food on offer - again - from the atrocious catering company that the club still amazingly employs.

Moaning aside, Posh started the second-half strongly earning a penalty after CMS was felled. At the time, and being in-front of the play, I was convinced he had his heels clipped, yet after seeing the highlights a day or so later, I soon realised it was highly dubious and the decision ultimately affected the outcome of the game. Super Craig dusted himself off and converted the penalty…just. The London Road end were now in as much of a full-voice as 4,500 could muster.

The opposition shut us up by equalising via a calamitous own goal from luckless centre-back Shane Blackett. Posh were once again undeterred and CMS netted his hat-trick with a mazy dribble and shot. But Rovers got their third back, nine minutes later, as former Posh loanee, Jeff Hughes struck after more woeful defending. A further nine minutes after that a wonderfully whipped Whelpdale cross was nodded in by Scott Rendell. Mixed in with the cheers was the biggest sigh of relief heard at London Road for some time as Posh looked to have closed out a pulsating encounter.

But had they? No, of course not, that would have been far too simple considering the context of the game. For the fourth time Rovers hit back with a quite stunning Rickie Lambert free-kick. I want football to be exciting but after the Bournemouth defeat about a decade ago I'd had enough of close games and luckily, unlike that occasion, Posh held-on for three points. I left the London Road via a pub and fortified by a very stiff drink made the long trip back to Portsmouth, but by God that 5-4 see-saw ride was worth it.

*Chris Dowsett*

* * * * *

**09/09/08**

Centre back Shane Blackett suffers a dislocated shoulder at the training ground and is expected to be ruled out of action for up to 12 weeks.

* * * * *

**11/09/08**

Gabriel Zakuani signs a three-month loan deal, not the previously advised one-month deal

* * * * *

**13/09/08**

## Northampton Town 1 - 1 Peterborough United

Larkin '43 Boyd '15

Att: 6,520 (1,424 away).

**Northampton Town:** Chris Dunn, Jason Crowe (-89'), Danny Jackman, Mark Hughes, Colin Larkin (-69'), Liam Davis (-46'), Mark Little, Karl Hawley, Ryan Gilligan (-78'), Liam Dolman, Luke Guttridge

Subs: Giles Coke (+78'), Leon Constantine (+69'), Andy Holt (+46'), Ian Henderson, Frank Fielding
**Peterborough United:** Joe Lewis, Russell Martin, Craig Morgan, Scott Rendell, George Boyd, Dean Keates, Craig Mackail-Smith, Paul Coutts (-78'), Jamie Day, Chris Whelpdale (-74'), Gabriel Zakuani
Subs: Chris Westwood, Micah Hyde (+78'), Shaun Batt, Dominic Green (+74'), Mark Tyler

My journey for this game started on the Wednesday at Johannesburg airport where I boarded a flight that included a 'quick' six hour stopover at the godforsaken hole that is Cairo Airport - not so quick when you have to crap in a hole in the wall and wait in the crowded airport lounge surrounded by a dozen African blokes in dresses, who for some reason must put their bare, flight addled feet, two centimetres from your nose as they lie across 19 waiting room chairs. I was met by mum and dad at Heathrow airport with a six-pack of Walkers Cheese and Onion and a bottle of diet Coke which I repaid by gassing them with a variety of 'flight farts' on the journey home.

Still it would be worth it and it was all kind of a bit surreal really. After being a season ticket holder for 25+ years and making reasonably regular trips home in my first couple of years away, the last three years had been Poshless as the creation of a little Kaasprodukte had arrived on the scene to introduce me to the financial constraints of fatherhood and stuff like responsibilities.

But this was Cobblers away. This was the one and after three long years of looking wistfully at posh.net every match day waiting for someone to slap one of those clapping emoticons (usually followed by 'McLean !!!' or 'CMS !!!') at the end of a thread to signal a goal. At last I would be there amongst a sea of blue righteousness, laughing at the funny people in the home areas with too many fingers who sleep with their sisters in a desperate attempt to boost their dwindling fan base.

So since mid July when the fixtures came out, I had been begging mum and dad for a bit of financial assistance - which was duly forthcoming - and had managed to scrape enough together to make even the ridiculous Rand/Pound exchange rate bow to my need for English beer, Melton Mowbray pork pies and a bit of Posh.

So Saturday came around and I met up with Mowlesy at 10am - who had been his usual sweet little darling self and organised me a ticket - to take my place on the PISA Express. Arriving at a pub in Higham Ferrers I settled down with a group of lads to have my first 'real' beer for three years. A pint of Adnams was duly despatched followed by a burp of lusty appreciation as I went to buy my first round of the day with what turned out to be approximately one months salary in South Africa.

More old faces turned up including Bob and Lord Truckwood (a couple of the old crowd I used to go to away games with) and we settled in for some proper drinking. Now for those of you who know me, I am not the world's best drinker, however I am one of the best in the world at two things. (1) necking pints in approximately 5 seconds and (2) chundering like a 13 year old who has just been on his first alcopop binge.

Sean, Bob and Mowlesy quickly got me a pint in, realising that I had suddenly got somewhat loud which usually signalled a drunken enough state to start the necking process and I duly despatched it in a time I was quite proud of considering my years out of the game. Then another was served and despatched in a time which did not do me justice. Sensing that a chunder was just around the corner and realising that I was beyond the point of arguing, the beasts moved in for the kill and made me neck another one before following me with howls of laughter as I rushed to the toilet, slammed the door (I can't remember the name of the pub, but I can remember the door was red for some reason?) dropped to the floor and barfed in glorious tribute to many away days of yesteryear.

'Refreshed' and ready for the game I boarded the coach. The lads on the coach were some of the older crowd and knew all the words to the Last Waltz and Posh We Are so the journey to the Sixfingerfields passed by in a blaze of beer addled Posh patriotism.

In the ground the atmosphere was actually the same as it always is for this derby. A couple of hundred 15 year old Wobbs fans standing up in the corner near the away and running one of their four index fingers across their throats in a threatening display of teenage intimidation, whilst being completely out-sung by Posh fans who were holding up six fingers in recognition of our foes genetic abnormalities.

For some reason Mowlesy presumed I would like to help him get the flag going around the away end and was less than impressed at the dexterity in which I completed this task as the flag was immediately ripped from my grasp but on this occasion - unlike previously when I have completed the same task - I felt really proud just being involved. Could have been the beer I suppose but after so many years away it gave me a buzz.

The game passed by for about 15 minutes or so, in which time it was plain to see that the class act on show was George Boyd. I had not seen him play before, but had heard everyone wibble on about him. Then bang - and I mean bang - he made space for himself inside the box and rifled one into the roof of the net to become an instant hero in my eyes.

The away end just erupted. The strange thing about the goal celebration was that it first went quiet for a second - as the goal came from nowhere - and then simultaneously we just went crazy as everyone did the whole mental 'epileptic spider' thing and hugged complete strangers before clambering back up off the floor and collapsing into their seats after realising that they are not fit enough to do the 'epileptic spider' with such abandon. It's such moments that make you realise that living in the sunshine is not the be all and end all of life – but Posh possibly is.

The rest is history, one of their foul cretins scuttled an equaliser in with a webbed foot just before half time, ex-Cambridge man Rendell missed a sitter near the end and we went home a little bit disappointed with a point we would have probably accepted before the game.

But for me, we could have lost by a cricket score and the day would have been still (almost) worth it. It was just great to be part of it all again. So, if in mid-winter, when you are sitting under a duvet freezing your nads offs and possibly considering emigrating to sunnier climes take my advice and don't do it, there's no Posh where you are going.

*Darin Lee*

*"I am left scratching my head again, wondering how we haven't collected three points, because we created a number of excellent opportunities in front of goal."*

*Darren Ferguson*

* * * * *

**20/09/08**

## Peterborough United 2 - 2 Tranmere Rovers

| | |
|---|---|
| Mackail-Smith '41 | Greenacre '7 |
| Zakuani '77 | Greenacre '30 |

Att: 5,735 (340 away).

**Peterborough United:** Joe Lewis, Russell Martin, Craig Morgan, Charlie Lee (-74'), Scott Rendell (-65'), George Boyd, Craig Mackail-Smith, Paul Coutts, Jamie Day, Chris Whelpdale, Gabriel Zakuani
Subs: Chris Westwood, Micah Hyde, Shaun Batt (+65'), Dominic Green (+74'), Mark Tyler
**Tranmere Rovers:** Danny Coyne, Andy Taylor, Ben Chorley, Ian Goodison, Antony Kay, Bas Savage, Ian Moore, Chris Greenacre, (-78'), Stephen Jennings, Edrissa Sonko, Ryan Shotton
Subs: George O'Callaghan, Gareth Edds, Chris Shuker, John Achterberg, Craig Curran (+78')

*"Our defending was not good enough in the first half. The first goal I haven't actually seen on television, but we definitely needed to be tighter to the guy crossing the ball, although it is an excellent header. The second goal was terrible defending, everyone left it to each other and that is not good enough."*

*Darren Ferguson*

* * * * *

**27/09/08**

## MK Dons 1 - 2 Peterborough United

Gerba '63 Mackail-Smith '73 (pen.)
Green '75

Att: 10,876.

**MK Dons:** Willy Guéret, Dean Lewington, Miguel Ángel Llera, Sean O'Hanlon, Mark Wright, Aaron Wilbraham (-38'), Carl Regan, Shaun Cummings, Ali Gerba, Alan Navarro, Peter Leven
Subs: Nathan Abbey, Jude Stirling, Jemal Johnson, Sam Baldock (+38'), Flavien Belson
**Peterborough United:** Joe Lewis, Russell Martin, Craig Morgan, Micah Hyde, George Boyd, Craig Mackail-Smith, Paul Coutts, Chris Whelpdale (-67'), Tommy Williams, Shaun Batt (-89'), Gabriel Zakuani (-22')
Subs: Chris Westwood (+22'), Charlie Lee (+89'), Scott Rendell, Dominic Green (+67'), Mark Tyler

There was always only one club I hated and that was of course the Wobbs. Then these nasty MK imposters were invented courtesy of a decision that went against everything the football league has ever stood for and they instantly became a club despised by all fair minded football fans.

Anyway despite vowing that I'd never go to a game there I've found my love of Posh overcoming any moral doubts and I've succumbed. My first visit took me to the hockey stadium - a perfect venue for them as it was hastily put together and not really worth it - and these past two seasons to the ASDA Memorial Bowl to watch, according to local radio and the imposters themselves - a local derby. I don't think so.

Last season we found a great pub and I saw no reason not to use said pub again, so the coach picked us up outside Ebs at the sensible hour of 9am. Needless to say there were complaints all over Peterborough of "Why do you have to leave so early for a 3 o'clock kick off" from the 'better halves' of the PISA members making the journey. The answer of course to that whine is that we were going via a hospice to tuck in the dying rather than the the scurrilous rumour that 10 pints pre-game are an integral part of a PISA coach trip.

Because of the 10 pints I am not sure I can in all honesty give a very accurate report of the game, (although it's not an important part of this publication so it doesn't really matter).

What I do remember is that we were allowed to surf the PISA flag by some quite friendly stewards. Unfortunately we POSH fans haven't a clue how to surf a flag, it seems to be the holding on to it and passing it on without letting go that seems to bamboozle most of us! *(No that makes no sense to me either, Editor)*

What I do remember is that the imposters could not deal with our secret weapon of the day: Forrest Gump aka Shaun Batt aka The Battman or whatever other moniker Posh fans choose to use.

I remember that their truly irritating goalkeeper - who's actually rather good to be honest - made a complete and utter fool of himself during the attack that led to our first goal by feigning serious injury, jumping up when he realised he couldn't stop what was happening and then pretending to be injured once again when he saw a penalty had been given.

What I also remember is that our second secret weapon of the day the young, small and waif like winger Dominic

Green powered (shinned) in the winner. He celebrated in front of 3,500 deliriously happy Posh fans who showed the imposters what it was like to actually support a side rather than come along because a friend got a freebie and it would be jolly nice to see what 'soccer' was like.

After lots of amusing gestures at locals who didn't really understand what had made us so happy it was back to Ebs to carry on the celebrations. Steve, over from Canada for the game, proved to Boozy and I that our power drinking days are over as he sank two pints to our one for a couple of hours before thankfully shooting off to some family do. "We'll be out all night celebrating," we told him, "we'll go to Charters from here then into town ending up at Rinaldos, Canters or Shanghai Sams." And then me and Boozy went home and were in bed by 9. Separate beds.

*Adi Mowles*

*"We didn't play as well as we could, but that was down to Peterborough who gave a really good display. I'd say they are the best League One side I have seen all season."*

*Roberto Di Matteo, MK Dons boss*

* * * * *

**28/09/08**

Russell Martin replaces Craig Morgan as team captain.

* * * * *

**30/09/08**

Mark Tyler joins Watford on an emergency loan deal.

* * * * *

**30/09/08**

| | | P | W | D | L | Pts |
|---|---|---|---|---|---|---|
| 1 | Oldham | 8 | 5 | 3 | 0 | 18 |
| 2 | Scunthorpe | 8 | 6 | 0 | 2 | 18 |
| | | | | | | |
| 10 | Posh | 8 | 3 | 2 | 3 | 11 |

# October

**02/10/08**

Fans attending Peterborough United's fixture with Leeds United on Saturday will have the opportunity to be tested for Chlamydia. The results will be published in the programme at the next home game.

* * * * *

**04/10/08**

Peterborough United 2 - 0 Leeds United
Boyd '47
Mackail-Smith '90

Att: 13,191 (4,058 away).

**Peterborough United:** Joe Lewis, Russell Martin, Craig Morgan, Micah Hyde, George Boyd, Craig Mackail-Smith, Paul Coutts (-83'), Tommy Williams, Shaun Batt, Dominic Green (-72'), Gabriel Zakuani
Subs: Chris Westwood, Charlie Lee (+83'), Scott Rendell, James McKeown, Chris Whelpdale (+72')
**Leeds United:** Casper Ankergren, Frazer Richardson, Jonathan Douglas, Rui Marques, Jermaine Beckford, Luciano Becchio, Jonny Howson (-56'), Fabian Delph (-67'), Andy Robinson, Paul Telfer, Aidan White (-74')
Subs: David Prutton, Neil Kilkenny (+67'), Ben Parker (+74'), Andy Hughes Robert Snodgrass (+56')

Landed at Stansted with four Italian friends who had never seen an English League game. So what better than to take them to Posh v Leeds United and the weekend started with me introducing them to a Friday night curry.

Up early for a full English and then off to the match and they could not believe how much freedom there is around the ground compared to Italy. Once inside they loved the atmosphere and the noise. And though they were freezing they even tried to join in with the singing. The score was the icing on the cake.

Thanks Posh, you did me proud.

*Davide Broccoli*

*"If we can beat Leeds we can beat anyone."*

*Darren Ferguson*

* * * * *

**07/10/08**

Football League Trophy

## Peterborough Utd 0 - 1 Dagenham & Redbridge

Nwokeji '65

Att: 2,644 (147 away).

**Peterborough United:** Joe Lewis, Russell Martin, Craig Morgan, Charlie Lee, Micah Hyde, George Boyd, Craig Mackail-Smith, Paul Coutts (-73'), Tommy Williams, Shaun Batt, Dominic Green (-56')
Subs: Scott Rendell (+73'), James McKeown, Chris Whelpdale (+56'), Sam Gaughran, Danny Andrew
**Dagenham & Redbridge:** Tony Roberts, Magnus Okuonghae, Glen Southam, Jon Nurse, Richard Graham (-69'), Mark Nwokeji (-86'), Scott Griffiths, Paul Benson (-46'), Anwar Uddin, Danny Foster, Peter Gain
Subs: Shane Huke (+69'), Ben Strevens (+46'), Arron Fray, Tommy Tejan-Sie (+86'), Ed Thompson

*Darragh McAnthony had a Wembley trip on his pre-season wish-list and as the chairman prides himself on getting what he wants, the disappointment at a first hurdle failure will be as immense in Marbella today as it was at London Road last night.*

*Posh were just a centre-back away from fielding the side that had beaten Leeds three days earlier, but they were a million miles away from a similar performance.*

*Dagenham & Redbridge, a much better side than the one beaten twice by Posh last season, defended superbly and pinched victory with a header by midget striker Mark Nwokeji which looped over the head of a six foot five inch goalkeeper midway through the second half.*

*Alan Swann*
*Evening Telegraph*

* * * * *

**09/10/09**

Posh lose another defender as Jamie Day faces nine months on the sidelines after being told he needs a back operation.

* * * * *

**11/10/08**

Walsall 1 - 2 Peterborough United

| | |
|---|---|
| Deeney '90 | Batt '2 |
| | Whelpdale '43 |

Att: 4,792.

**Walsall:** Rene Gilmartin, Paul Boertien (-58'), Stephen Roberts, Anthony Gerrard, Stephen Hughes, Chris Palmer, Dwayne Mattis, Jabo Ibehre (-79'), Michael Ricketts, Richard Taundry, Marco Reich (-57')
Subs: Rhys Weston, Tom Cox, Ishmel Demontagnac (+58'), Alex Nicholls (+79'), Troy Deeney (+57')
**Peterborough United:** Joe Lewis, Russell Martin, Charlie Lee, Micah Hyde, George Boyd, Craig Mackail-Smith, Paul Coutts (-69'), Chris Whelpdale (-61'), Kieran Charnock, Tommy Williams, Shaun Batt
Subs: Shane Blackett, Aaron McLean (+61'), Dean Keates (+69'), James McKeown, Dominic Green

A home game at last! Always good when Posh play at one of my closest grounds, and also one of the friendliest clubs around - with the bonus of Balti pies. Halesowen to Walsall is a good 12 miles, so I set out early, making sure I had a good supply of faggots with grey peas, scratchings and Grorty pudding, for the long haul across the Black Country .

Arriving at the ground the first stop is the excellent Saddlers Club. A bit of a shock though when the guy on the door said he wasn't letting any more Posh fans in, as there were already so many there wouldn't be room for their own fans! He relented though, as there were only two of us at the door, so in I went, got a pint, and had a look around. I soon found the dedicated drinkers in a corner; Adi, Nick from Brizzle and, of course, Boydie's No 1 fan Brian, who claims to enjoy the odd shandy, but who had a very impressive collection of empty glasses in front of him. He reckoned it was a frame up, but I'm not so sure.

After a very enjoyable hour or so of banter with the locals (it was obvious they were a bit more worried about Posh this time), we all wandered into the ground. Plenty of noise from our end, not really that much from the Saddlers fans as the teams came out and warmed up.

I'm always a bit nervous when we play the Saddlers. We've had some bad results against them, and the last time I was here watching Posh, we got hammered 5 – 0, with two men sent off. I spent quite a bit of that game with my head in my hands, wondering how even Keith Alexander could make the football uglier than this. Not my last time in the ground though. That was standing in the centre circle, playing music for the Jockey Morris Men, while eight sides taking part in an Inter Faith football tournament practiced around us. Well, what else is there to do on a Tuesday evening? But I digress.

Their fans have been a bit hacked off with Posh over the years too, though, mainly because of our odd habit of running off with pairs of their players (Martin O'Connor and Scott Houghton, then of course Chris Westwood and Dean Keates).

The game got underway and for once we got off to a great start at Walsall . Only 90 secs gone and Shaun Batt put us ahead. (I felt pleased for the guy in the stand wearing the Batman outfit. It must have seemed a great idea in the morning, but if Shaun had had a mare, he may just have regretted it). I texted a Walsall supporting mate of mine, (as he'd done to me five times at the previous game). He surprised me by saying he wasn't in the ground, but that Sky reckoned Walsall were well on top!

Chris Whelpdale put us two up (I looked around in vain for anyone in a whelp costume). Posh were on fine form, gave the woodwork some hammer, and wasted several chances to go further ahead. Walsall's very late goal was only a consolation, and did nothing to disguise the fact that Posh were much, much better than them on the day, and for once I left their ground happy!

There is a bit of a postscript. The following Wednesday I was in a pub quiz in the Waggon and Horses in Halesowen. Question master Keith is a Saddlers fan and he announced that, "for one week only there is a 10 point penalty for any teams that include Peterborough supporters!"

As it turned out, it made no odds. Our quiz team were on right Walsall form that night.

*Gary Chilvers*

It's not very often I drive to away games, I'd rather have a dozen pints as generally, over the years, it has been easier watching Posh drunk rather than sober. This season I've driven to a few matches as I enjoy watching this team so much that I like to remember the football rather than down pint after pint in the hope that the hangover obliterates any memory of the previous day's game.

A lack of communication between me and my missus meant she had agreed to us going to a wedding reception in the evening. She normally drives to these things but in a moment of weakness I agreed to be the designated driver for our trip to Welwyn Garden City. Generally I only let women drive me when I am pissed. Anyway if she was drunk I might get some lurrve later on.

The Bescot is one of the easier grounds to get to so we set off at 10am confident that we'd reach the superb Saddlers Club in time for the bar opening and their fantastic food to be cooked and ready. As you can see even when not drinking my thoughts are on the two most important pre-match rituals.

I met up with an old mate of mine, Potton Matt, who now lives in Brum and after my first orange and lemonade I was gagging for a pint but more importantly I could see the balti pies and chips were ready and calling my name.

Suitably nourished the talk soon turned to the game and the disastrous news that Craig Morgan was out - playing for some third world country - and Chris Westwood was injured and the prospect of Charlie Lee at 5″3 and Kieran Charnock as our central defence wasn't inspiring confidence. Charlie I could live with as he'd come to us as a Tottenham reserve team centre back but young Kieran had previously taken the Bruce Lee role in a remake of the kung fu classic *Penalty Area Or Not I Will Kick Your Head Off* at the Scunthorpe Multiplex. We all respected the fact that he was young and inexperienced and none of us would have told him face-to-face that he wasn't very good as he looks pretty damm hard, but after Fergie's very public condemnation of his assault at Scunny we were surprised to see him wearing a Posh shirt again.

I could feel the onset of doom and gloom rapidly approaching so I made my way over to the food area and in an effort to console myself I enjoyed a second balti pie - they weren't very big, honest! Things always seem better after a pie so with a possibly misguided sense of optimism I made my way to the away end and joined another sizeable Posh turnout, settled down with someone elses programme and awaited the Charnock show.

I'm not going to do a match report as they can be found elsewhere and written a lot more betterer than my efforts but my God we started like a house on fire. CMS was out of this world. The turn he did on the touchline to set up the first goal for Whelps took the breath away and after the 90 mins we walked away with a thoroughly deserved victory though the last few minutes were a bit scary.

However, the day belonged to the central partnership. Charlie Lee was outstanding and on any other day would have walked away with MoM but then on any other day Kieran Charnock wouldn't have given such a assured display. Indeed, up till then we were waiting for a display that would prove he'd even played football before! He was a mixture of Alan Hansen, John Charles and Chris Turner so immense was he in his total dominance over the man mountain Walsall had up front.

The journey back was full of excited chat and the discussion in the car and on Radio Scum was full of praise, the CMS turn and general performance, Charlie Lee's superb performance, Russell Martin being a great signing and the superb reception Dean Keates got from the home supporters - but time and time again the conversation turned to young Kieran.

Was Capello at the game and if so was Charnock due a call up? Would Fergie Snr be in touch as that Vidic was obviously nowhere near as good? How on earth would Morgs get back in the side?

We arrived back in Peterborough with all these questions still reverberating around our heads and I went home, picked up my missus for the trip to the wedding reception. My devious plan worked a treat because exactly 9 months after Kieran Charnock's finest Posh hour Caz and I will have another young Posh supporter in our midst - told you I got some lurrving when she was drunk!

The way to finish this story for those who don't know would be for Kieran Charnock to have become a regular in the side and then been snapped up by Barcelona for a multi-million pound transfer fee.

He ended up on loan at Accrington Stanley. Bless.

*Adi Mowles*

* * * * *

**18/10/08**

## Carlisle United 3 -3 Peterborough United

| | |
|---|---|
| Graham '20 | Lee '34 |
| Graham '50 | Mackail-Smith '60 (pen.) |
| Kavanagh '52 | Mackail-Smith '90 |

Att: 6,074 (377 away).

**Carlisle United:** Ben Alnwick, David Raven, Evan Horwood, Danny Livesey, Danny Graham (-79'), Danny Carlton (-72'), Luke Joyce, Cleveland Taylor (-85'), Simon Hackney, Richard Keogh, Graham Kavanagh
Subs: Ben Williams, Jennison Myrie-Williams (+85'), Josh Gowling, Gary Madine (+79'), Jeff Smith (+72')
**Peterborough United:** Joe Lewis, Russell Martin, Charlie Lee, Micah Hyde (-53'), George Boyd, Craig Mackail-Smith, Paul Coutts, Chris Whelpdale (-57'), Tommy Williams (-53'), Shaun Batt, Gabriel Zakuani
Subs: Shane Blackett (+53') (-89'), Craig Morgan (+53'), Aaron McLean (+57'), James McKeown, Dominic Green

I'm not your average Posh fan. I have never lived in the city or remotely close to it but I've been avid for a good 11 years or so and watching the Posh has stuck with me. Despite the long distances and the money I've spent to watch Posh home and away I love it, even if that does mean travelling to Carlisle away.

Now I've been to some games that you might label as stupid; Burton Albion away in the cup after travelling from the north-west in a horribly hungover state, or Stockport on my girlfriend's birthday without telling her. This season I decided to trek from Portsmouth to watch Posh at Carlisle. Usually when the fixtures come out, this fixture is met with groans but having lived in Lancaster for the previous three years and missing the Morecambe game last season, I felt I could combine a weekend of drinking in my former stamping ground and watching the Mighty Posh maintain their unbeaten streak. The plan couldn't fail, could it?

The Friday that I left began well, no train delays meant a comfortable journey plus a wallet full of cash for what was set to be a great weekend. However, on arrival in Lancashire's county town it soon became apparent that I would be sleeping on my mates' floor unless I got lucky and found a student hussy to take me in and snuggle up to. A horrendous amount of drink was consumed, and that all but eradicated my chances of a bed that night so, alas, I spent what was left of the night on the floor. After 3 hours sleep and a journey to the train station in the pissing rain, I was ready for Carlisle. Standing on the platform, with the world's worst cup of tea in my hands, I set eyes on the most insanely beautiful honey I have ever witnessed. Still full of drunken bravado I struck up conversation but, quite predictably, she didn't hang around. The Lancaster – Carlisle stretch of railway takes in some beautiful countryside and some outstanding views of the Lake

District; however that day of all days I was absolutely in no mood to sit and marvel and planned to fall asleep in an attempt to clear the now worsening hangover. Of course, as the weekend was to pan out this was not possible, and I spent the hour long journey in the company of a single mother who should never been allowed to have offspring, let alone two of the little horrors, and that really was the sign of things to come.

On arrival in Carlisle I was given some frankly terrible directions to the designated pub and found the place about half an hour later and then only after taking advice from some very depressed coppers. Once inside, and meeting with Nick and Keith, hair of the dog was a necessity, along with some food, at a wonderfully under-inflated price. I love the North! Later fellow Posh company joined from Peterborough and Leeds, as well as Kev from Edinburgh and his fantastically drunken friend, Darren.

Once at the game we were treated to a lively start with a clearance off the line and Carlisle hitting the woodwork. The game sprung into life as the Cumbrians deservedly took the lead after 20 minutes, but Posh hit back a quarter of an hour later, with a Lee header from a Martin corner. The interval arrived as torrential rain lashed down and hardy Posh fans were politely reminded to be 'careful on the steps, as they may be wet'.

Whatever Fergie said at half-time didn't work as Posh promptly found themselves 3-1 down. Firstly Joe Lewis spilled a weak shot for Danny Graham to score his second, and two minutes later Posh's defence opened up and stood back to allow the evergreen Graham Kavanagh to notch his first for the club. It looked like game over, and once again I questioned the logic of making the trip but this Posh side never know when they are beaten. Eight minutes later CMS converted a penalty after a handball and we were back in it. After half an hour of huffing and puffing, Posh looked out of ideas as they tried to make a breakthrough, but the fourth official gave us hope when he signalled four minutes of additional time. The first minute of the four was the turning point as substitute Shane Blackett being carried off injured with a dislocated shoulder. My esteemed friend Jimbo was positively outraged as he feared missing the last train back to Huntingdon, and he let Blackett know about it. His outrage soon turned to pure ecstasy as, with the last kick of the game, CMS raced onto a Charlie Lee punt to equalise and maintain the unbeaten run.

I don't remember much of the celebrations apart from hugging lots of grown men I'd never met before and jumping up and down in a frenzy. I don't think it had really hit me that we had only got an equaliser at lowly Carlisle, but it felt like so much more. After being molested by a very strange local, congratulating me on a point, I headed back to Lancaster via a pub and got my head down for the night.

The next day I got to the station to get my 9am train. But there was nobody at the train station and when I finally found somebody I was informed that no trains would be leaving until 11, and that getting back to the South Coast would take all day! From Lancaster to Preston then Stafford onto Banbury a rail replacement bus to Didcot to Southampton Central with the world and his wife and finally missing my connection and only arriving home after nearly twelve hours of epic travel.

I'd travelled the length and breadth of the country, and for what? A crucial point at Carlisle of course!

*Chris Dowsett*

* * * * *

**21/10/08**

## Peterborough Utd 0 - 0 Brighton & Hove Albion

Att:5,772 (578 away).

**Peterborough United:** Joe Lewis, Russell Martin, Craig Morgan, Charlie Lee, George Boyd, Craig Mackail-Smith, Paul Coutts, Chris Whelpdale (-62'), Tommy Williams, Shaun Batt (-80'), Gabriel Zakuani
Subs: Micah Hyde, Aaron McLean (+62'), James McKeown, Dominic Green (+80'), Sam Gaughran
**Brighton & Hove Albion:** Michel Kuipers, Adam El-Abd, Steven Thomson, Kevin McLeod (-80'), Matt Richards, Colin Hawkins, Glenn Murray, Adam Virgo, Tommy Elphick, Joe Anyinsah, Robbie Savage (-89')
Subs: Andrew Whing, Dean Cox, Kevin Thornton (+89'), Dave Livermore (+80'), Tommy Fraser

That was rubbish. Brighton arrived with absolutely no intention of trying to win and put 10 men behind the ball and parked Robbie Savage's hair and make-up bag in front of the goal.

Posh dominated possession and passed the ball around nicely but I can't recall a clear shot on goal.

*Paul Mitchell*

* * * * *

**25/10/08**

## Peterborough United 4 - 0 Huddersfield Town

McLean '12
Boyd '24
Whelpdale '55
McLean '63

Att: 7,058 (949 away).

**Peterborough United:** Joe Lewis, Russell Martin, Craig Morgan, Charlie Lee, Aaron McLean (-64'), George Boyd (-67'), Craig Mackail-Smith, Paul Coutts (-67'), Chris Whelpdale, Tommy Williams, Gabriel Zakuani
Subs: Micah Hyde (+67'), James McKeown, Sergio Torres (+67'), Shaun Batt (+64'), Dominic Green
**Huddersfield Town:** Matt Glennon, Andy Holdsworth, Ian Craney, Nathan Clarke, Jon Worthington, Michael Flynn, Jim Goodwin, Robbie Williams, Gary Roberts, Chris Lucketti (-89'), Liam Dickinson
Subs: Joe Skarz, Michael Collins, Phil Jevons (+61'), Andy Butler, Daniel Broadbent

Just as the man who has endured the famine may celebrate the harvest, so may the man who has stood among 3,000 other hardy souls on a Tuesday night in February, watching Barry Fry's Peterborough United kick and rush their way to a 0-0 stalemate with Northern Industrial Town FC bask in the warm glow of a 4-0 win over a team once considered our superiors.

The name of Huddersfield will be forever etched into the memory of a good few thousand Posh supporters. On that famous day back in '92 we were the victors. Pinpoint precision from the right foot of Barnes, a mighty dive from a temporary hero - and a firm, accurate header that would elevate him to almost mythical status among the wide-eyed supporters. They were going to Wembley. The home of football. To watch their team. A story to be passed down through the generations. And so may today's encounter with yesterday's quarry be another landmark in the brief history of Peterborough United Football Club.

To those unfortunate followers who could not be at London Road today, my friends, I cannot lie, this was a quite incredible success. From the very first minute it was apparent that there would only be one outcome. The naysayers of the local press affiliated to each week's chosen opposition may write us off as a millionaire's plaything; a result of over-inflated transfer fees and market dominance, but that is both untrue and an injustice to the skill and judgement of Darren Ferguson, Kevin Russell, Barry Fry and Darragh MacAnthony.

This is a squad thoughtfully assembled from the cream of talent in the lower leagues. Take Craig Mackail-Smith; a scrawny youth, released by St Albans Town, but so strong of character he held his head high and impressed at Arlesey, enough to earn a transfer to Dagenham, where his relentless effort and eye for goal earned him a ticket to league football. Charlie Lee; a product of the youth system at Tottenham Hotspur. A much-fancied youngster whose passion and commitment were not rewarded with equal measures of faith and loyalty. Paul Coutts; a midfielder plucked from the Highland League. A lad with a troubled past, taken under the wing of masterful Micah Hyde and transformed into a visionary ball-player. Such composure is rarely seen in one so young. And then there's George Boyd. One will never know quite how such folk heroes as Denis Emery and Tommy Robson would have coped in today's game, so to proclaim any player as the greatest ever is mere bluff and bluster. But what can be claimed - and may well be disputed - is that the lank-haired, lackadaisical-at-a-glance steal from Stevenage is the most talented footballer to have graced the PE2 turf in his generation.

Today was no one-off. Once more Boyd toyed with his adversaries, seemingly more happy when given two men to beat rather than one, opening up chance after chance for his grateful comrades. 4-0 was an understatement. A scoreline which flattered a bewildered Huddersfield Town. We are witnessing a rebirth. A ray of light at the end of a gloomy ten-year-tunnel. This is a team that could go all the way. This is a time to appreciate how lucky we are. This truly is a time to be proud to be Posh.

*Jack Thorpe*

Foca is a little Turkish fishing village that is similar to Mousehole in Cornwall, similar in size, similar in desirability, and similar in just how bloody isolated it is. It is my wife's idea of the perfect retirement destination. My take on this has been to invest in such solid retirement vehicles as Northern Rock, HBOS, and Woolworths, all of which should have provided 'options' when retirement can no longer be deferred. Of course the real reason for me not committing to the dreams of 'her indoors' will be understood by everyone who reads this book: "how can I get to watch the Posh whilst living in Asia?"

What as all this got to do with a bleak Saturday in October? Well this was the day when I was going to have the opportunity to test my future travel arrangements. After a week of holidaying in the sun (house hunting) I had booked to leave Foca on the Saturday, with the intention of seeing just what was possible using public transport. My early enthusiasm had been dented when a mid-week visit to the local internet café had provided the news that we had managed only a measily two points from a safe six point haul against lowly Brighton and Carlisle.

At 6am I was climbing onboard the first Dolmus (clapped out old minibus) out of Foca. Along with the Mrs and a couple of cases, I was travelling with a crowd of what appeared to be the local peasant element - unless of course the entire membership of the Wobbs supporters club were in Turkey that day. An bumpy hour later we pulled into a large carpark where we were due to transfer to a modern coach service that linked Izmir City to the airport. 7am on the outskirts of Izmir, and Posh were only the second best supported team in the carpark; With my blue Posh sponsored top clearly visible we managed to bump into the local branch of the Galatasary supporters club preparing to set off on the long road trip to Istanbul. They seemed more bemused than anything, and we safely boarded the coach for the 50 minute journey to the airport. The ticket price was cheaper for us Brits than for the locals, which must be a first!

We arrived at the airport in good time, and eventually found ourselves at the front of a bizarre queue of couples waiting to board the Turkish Cypriot Airlines flight to Heathrow. Paddy, the loud foul mouthed Irishman immediately behind us, was accompanied by a fragile looking Turkish wife, who quite clearly would rather be missing the flight. The big women behind Paddy , who looked like Vanessa Feltz in a Middlesbro footie top, was being worshipped by her Turkish toyboy, and another Anglo-Turkish couple were arguing over which passport they should use. This was the only international flight due out that morning, so the whole place was pretty empty. 10am saw the aircraft land, and by 10.20 we were airborne and heading for London.

Oh the advantage of time zones - just before noon GMT the aircraft was making its final approach as it followed the Thames from east to west. The Valley, The Emirates, Wembley Stadium, Wimbledon, Griffin Park, all came into view one after another and then bump, bump, bump, and Mickey Mouse's favourite airline had completed yet another cost effective journey. Hand luggage only saves a huge amount of time, and by 12.30 we were out of the airport and heading towards Peterborough.

Two hours later we were trying to get into the ground from the Moy's End of the Glebe Road and got turned away - lower tier full - that was utter bollocks as everyone knows you can access all parts of the Glebe from here. We then found ourselves in a long queue outside the main Glebe Road entrance. Two turnstiles were operating at a snails pace while the other two sat in silence awaiting the occasional season ticket holder. It was about three minutes to kick-off when we reached the turnstile. The operator was saying to her colleague that there were less than 20 tickets left, I could see that that would be problems for some of the 90+ who were still outside. Leaping up the stairs we made the top tier just as the players were about to kick off. Hunting for G157 &G158 we found it occupied by a couple of likely lads who were somewhat reluctant to vacate the seats. I stood my ground; their mates were questioning whether we had season tickets; and most behind us didn't give a toss just so long as we stopped obscuring their view. Reluctantly, and after some unnecessary bad-mouthing, they moved to their allocated seats. During all this commotion there was not a steward in sight As we all remember, this was one of our better home performances of the season, and we ran out comfortable 4 - 0 winners.

So what did the day teach me? It showed that it will be just about possible to commute from a Turkish fishing village in my retirement. It also reinforced the view that when making a 4,000 mile journey, experiencing different cultures and using various forms of public transport problems are most likely to occur once PUFC get involved.

Finally, if you recognise yourself as the plonker who was determined to sit in my seat you now know why I was so abrupt, I'd been travelling since 4am.

*The Village Idiot*

* * * * *

**28/10/08**

## Crewe Alexandra 1 - 1 Peterborough United

Pope '88 McLean '14

Att: 3,699.

**Crewe Alexandra:** Steve Collis, Danny O'Donnell, Michael O'Connor (-60'), Joel Grant, George Abbey (-81'), Byron Moore, Shaun Miller (-72'), James Bailey, Clayton Donaldson, John Brayford, Dennis Lawrence
Subs: Steven Schumacher (+60'), Anthony Elding, Calvin Zola, Mark Carrington (+81'), Tom Pope (+72')

**Peterborough United :** Joe Lewis, Russell Martin, Craig Morgan, Charlie Lee (-71′), Aaron McLean Goal (-82′), George Boyd, Craig Mackail-Smith, Paul Coutts, Chris Whelpdale (-63′), Tommy Williams, Gabriel Zakuani
Subs: Micah Hyde (+71′), James McKeown, Sergio Torres (+82′), Shaun Batt (+63′), Dominic Green

This was the most ill-thought out journey since Mark Thatcher's decision to take a short cut through the Sahara in the Paris-Dakar Rally. It was a night when my sons realised that their dad really does deserve all the abuse he receives on a daily basis.

A trip to Crewe on a Tuesday night was a half-term treat (I really can't believe I have never won a 'Father of the Year' Trophy) for Andrew and a break from studying at Uni for Mike. It was a busman's holiday for me. I like to spend one match a season mingling with the terrace intellect and wit, as well as Messrs Mowles and Donnelly.

Mike's at Birmingham, which is on the way to Crewe, so what could possibly go wrong? Nothing apart from leaving the Boro stupidly late at 3pm, hitting the M6 at rush hour, spending two hours driving through the middle of Brum, following signs for the away supporters at Crewe to a dead industrial estate, parking the car in a hurry and not seeing a pay and display sign (£30 towards another 'kin speed camera), missing the kick-off by 20 mins and not getting into the ground before Aaron McLean's early goal.

Oh well at least we were certain to score more and win against the worst team in the league. We had after all played like Brazil a few days earlier in thumping Huddersfield. But no, Posh were largely hopeless, Shaun Batt was large and hopeless, and Sergio Torres wouldn't have attracted more venom from the old git behind me, if he'd turned up in a Northampton shirt with 'Maradona' emblazoned on the back. 'The bloody useless foreigner' was eventually punished for giving away possession once too often as Crewe claimed a last-gasp equaliser with a mis-hit shot from a centre-back playing up front.

Brilliant. Got back home at 2am after promising that the next school holiday would be spent at Skegness.

*Alan Swann*

* * * * *

**31/10/08**

| | | P | W | D | L | Pts |
|---|---|---|---|---|---|---|
| 1 | Scunthopre | 14 | 9 | 2 | 3 | 29 |
| 2 | Millwall | 14 | 9 | 2 | 3 | 29 |
| | | | | | | |
| 8 | Posh | 14 | 6 | 5 | 3 | 23 |

# *November*

**01/11/08**

## Peterborough United 2 - 0 Hereford United

Mackail-Smith '35
Mackail-Smith '68

Att: 6,087 (188 away)

**Peterborough United:** Joe Lewis, Russell Martin, Craig Morgan, Charlie Lee, Aaron McLean (-76'), George Boyd, Craig Mackail-Smith, Paul Coutts, Chris Whelpdale (-22'), Tommy Williams, Gabriel Zakuani
Subs: Chris Westwood, Micah Hyde, James McKeown, Sergio Torres (+76'), Shaun Batt (+22')
**Hereford United:** Darren Randolph, Richard Rose, Toumani Diagouraga, Kris Taylor, Ben Smith, Steve Guinan, Bradley Hudson-Odoi, Clint Easton (-84'), Sam Gwynne (-69'), Karl Broadhurst, Bruno N'Gotty (-9')
Subs: Craig Samson, Stephen O'Leary, Andy Williams (+69'), Matt Done (+84'), Dean Beckwith

The day the fixtures came out there were those who looked to see when we were playing Leeds, others looked for Leicester or Wobbs. Me? I looked to see when Hereford were due to play at London Road. Hereford are my second team, both of my parents were at Edgar Street when HUFC famously knocked Newcastle out of the FA Cup and I'd been lucky enough to see both sides promoted last season.

Having had plenty of stick in Ebs, we walked to the ground and stood on the London Road terrace. Hereford went into the game on a low ebb, having found League One a lot harder than League Two and were near to the bottom of the table. It looked like they were due for a pasting.

I was pleasantly surprised by how Hereford played as the week before Brighton had been to London Road and I don't think Joe Lewis touched the ball all game as they defended with 11 men for 90 minutes. There was none of this from HUFC, the team played good football and started to threaten going forward - impressive when you realise Steve Guinan is about as old as my Dad!

Posh won a penalty and to call it controversial would be kind. Karl Broadhurst was accused of handball and it was duly given. Darren Randolph saved it but CMS put the rebound in. Hereford had less cutting edge than a very blunt thing with no cutting edge so any chance of getting something from the game disappeared at that moment, although they did have a couple of shots in the second half.

CMS added a second goal after half time, from a rare header when the Hereford defence decided to stop marking the opposition and that really was that. I'm rather glad that the two sides won't be in the same division next season, as it's bloody weird wanting both sides to win a match and neither to lose!

*Daniel Ferguson-Thomas*

* * * * *

**06/11/08**

Midfielder Micah Hyde is placed on the transfer list

* * * * *

**09/11/08**

FA Cup First Round

AFC Hornchurch 0 - 1 Peterborough United

Mackail-Smith '90

Att: 3,000.

**AFC Hornchurch:** Dale Brightly, Donny Barnard, Lee Brown (-89'), John Purdie (-88'), Mark Goodfellow, Andy Tomlinson, Frankie Curley, Mark Janney, Kris Lee (-63'), Dean Green, Elliot Styles
Subs: Simon Parker (+63'), Billy Coyne, Lee Hodges (+89'), Ross Wall, Mitchell Stuart-Evans, Jim McFarlane (+88'), Michael Bowditch
**Peterborough United:** Joe Lewis, Russell Martin, Craig Morgan, Aaron McLean, George Boyd, Dean Keates, Paul Coutts, Tommy Williams, Sergio Torres (-60'), Dominic Green (-60'), Gabriel Zakuani
Subs: Chris Westwood, Craig Mackail-Smith (+60'), James McKeown, Shaun Batt (+60'), Lewis Webb, Sam Gaughran, Danny Blanchett

So Posh had another lovely trip to a non-league club. The rosy-faced locals - many of whom had never previously been within a mile of the ground - clutch tin foil imitations of the FA Cup before asking their way down to the local athletics track to watch a group of bakers, builders and general oddjobbers take on the might of Peterborough United.

Due to the fact that Saturday saw West Ham taking on Everton at nearby Upton Park, this prestigious cup-tie, and I use that term in the loosest possible sense, was switched to a 2pm kick off on the Sunday at the newish Hornchurch Stadium.

Unlike many non-league clubs Posh have faced in the past, Hornchurch acted with a fair amount of decorum. A more than generous ticket allocation, some 1,500 allowed to Posh when in truth only 1,100 travelled - although where those extra characters could have been housed is frankly anyone's guess.

I met the rest of our small travelling party at Kings Cross and a brief trip on the Underground found us at Tower Bridge and then on to Wetherspoons on Liberty Square. With it being Remembrance Sunday, the pub was heaving with suited n' booted people ready to pay their respects. We were more bothered about how many ales we could get down our necks between the hours of 9.45am and 1.15pm

As we discussed the various topics of the day - the merits of resting our star players etc - dear old Boozy Baz looked intrigued at the building in front of him. He looked in amazement at the architecture and the sheer history of it. He casually turned to me and asked me what the building was and was it a famous one. As beer had been drunk I wondered if he was, shall we say, pulling ones todger.

"No, straight up", was his reply.

"It's the Tower of London you arse, arguably one of the most well-known landmarks in our great capital."

"Oh I've never seen it from this angle before."

Nine pints and a short later it was time to say our goodbyes and make our way to Upminster and the hovel, sorry, home of our non league opponents. We made kick off just, going through a turnstile that was similar to one of the barriers you'd see at a hastily arranged village fete

The pitch was poor, it had more bobbles than a 60-year old jumper and more mud than a pig could ever roll in. The wind was so strong that the modern day light football was in danger of floating off and disappearing like the balloons the locals had released.

The game itself was shit – no other word can describe it. With the previous management 0-0 would have been predictable, and welcomed. More money, a replay and everyone's happy. Thankfully those days are long gone. The first half provided a solitary free kick from Russell Martin well tipped over the bar by the amateur keeper and that was it.

Hornchurch had kindly provided the away contingent with a beer tent that had a capacity barely greater than the rather sad looking standing terrace next to the discus/hammer net. In fact the four toilets behind the goal could accommodate more than the beer tent. To be honest it wouldn't have been the end of the world if the travelling masses had been allowed to stay in there rather than watch the second half. The atmosphere was certainly a lot better.

Posh struggled though to hold on as Hornchurch had the wind, the slope and the bobbles in the second half. They, like Posh, huffed and puffed but neither looked capable of scoring. Thankfully Craig Mackail-Smith came on for the last 30 minutes and looked as if he was the only one with the ability to change the game. With the seconds ticking away George Boyd fired in a low scuffer towards the goalkeeper who spilt it, like his morning tea after a heavy night on the pop, straight at the feet of Craig Mackail-Smith,who gleefully poked it into the net from six yards. Over went the fences in non-league fashion and Posh were through to face either Tranmere or Accrington in the next round.

The locals wished us well for the rest of the competition and their whole attitude towards our visit was generous and one that did them credit. You only have to see how the likes of Droylesden do the reputation of their non-league brothers no good at all.

We were back on the train and back into Tower Bridge and the Liberty Bounds boozer by 5pm where for a good long while we warmed our wotsits and spoke yet more bollocks. We had won what was easily the worst game of the season to date. Probably the worst game of the season that anyone will witness and one of the top five worst I've watched in the 20+ years I've followed the club. However, the Guinness was cold, the company excellent and it was just another great away day watching Peterborough United.

*Mark Shepherd*

* * * * *

**11/11/09**

Joe Lewis is called into the England U21 Squad.

Paul Coutts wins a first call-up to Scottish U21 squad.

Craig Morgan is named in the Welsh squad to face Denmark.

* * * * *

**15/11/08**

## Yeovil Town 0 - 1 Peterborough United
McLean '36

Att: 4,001

**Yeovil Town:** Josh Wagenaar, Terry Skiverton, Gareth Owen , Darren Way, Danny Schofield, Craig Alcock (-85'), Paul Warne (-62'), Gary Roberts , Gifton Noel-Williams , Lee Peltier, Nathan Smith (-79')
Subs: Nathan Jones (+79'), Terrell Forbes, Andy Welsh (+85'), Aidan Downes (+62'), Kieran Murtagh
**Peterborough United:** Joe Lewis, Russell Martin, Craig Morgan, Charlie Lee (-75'), Aaron McLean, George Boyd, Dean Keates, Craig Mackail-Smith (-89'), Tommy Williams, Sergio Torres (-82'), Gabriel Zakuani
Subs: Chris Westwood (+89'), James McKeown, Paul Coutts (+75'), Shaun Batt (+82'), Dominic Green

I combined this game with an impromptu tour of the Avonmouth area as I looked for Nick's (Bristol Posh) house, as I'd arranged to give him a lift to the match.

Once I'd found him, we set off back to the M5, and down to Yeovil. I'd got a route (sort of) worked out, but it was encouraging to find ourselves following the team coach. Either we were on the right road, or Posh were lost too. Luckily it was the former, so we arrived and parked up, and strolled across to the ground. I tried to get a ticket in the same part of the ground as Brizzle, but I was told I had to stand; Nick was told he shouldn't have had a ticket for the stand anyway as that was only for kids and pensioners - and stag parties including a bunch of blokes in DMac suits and a journalist dressed as a French maid.

From there it was over to the beer tent though some Yeovil fans told us it wasn't a beer tent and the club had informed them that it was a hospitality marquee. Either way they were getting shot of some Polish beer at a quid a pint. Apparently they'd got it in for local Polish workers but they all drank the draught beers the club had on sale. A few minutes later the pasties turned up so I had a late breakfast. At the other end of the bar stood Trevor Peacock who played Jim in the Vicar of Dibley. Amazingly nobody asked him to have a drink to see if he would answer "No, no, no, no, no; no, no, yes. The locals were a friendly bunch, and we had a bit of a chat with them about Scott Rendell among other things. A trier, but not that good seemed to be their opinion. Seemed fair.

In to the ground and on to the terrace via the toilets, which were decorated with vases of flowers. The flowers were artificial, but still an unusual touch. A decent number of Poshies had made the trip given the distance but they were a bit quiet for an away crowd. Posh started quite brightly and George Boyd put a good shot in which came back off the post. The next action came when a couple of apparently brain-dead chavs were chucked out for giving Nazi salutes (locals or passing Millwall supporters depending on your choice of report). The early pressure told as McLean gave us the lead and - in what ITV reckoned was the best moment of the match - ran to the stand to have his head dusted by the French Maid. It turned out they were right and that was the last real highspot other than a fine save from Joe Lewis.

I left quite happy with three points after an ordinary performance and went out to find Nick so we could set off home. It turned out that he seemed to have been adopted by a local girl who trailed him back to the car park. Difficult to see what was in it for her, really!

There is only one way out of the Yeovil car park, so we sat in a queue for what seemed hours waiting to get on to the main road. It's a shame that the hospitality marquee was unavailable to away fans after the match as an hour watching the football reports while the traffic died down would have been far more enjoyable.

Once on the road, though, we had no hold ups. Just as well, as Nick was anxious to get back in time to watch Strictly Come Dancing. As many have said before, "Hmmmmmmmm".

*Gary Chilvers*

* * * * *

**18/11/08**

Gillingham midfielder Andrew Crofts joins on-loan.

Striker Scott Rendell rejoins Cambridge United on-loan until January.

* * * * *

**22/11/08**

## Peterborough United 2 - 1 Colchester United

Mackail-Smith '45 — Platt '61

Boyd '63

Att: 7,401 (513 away).

**Peterborough United:** Joe Lewis, Russell Martin, Craig Morgan, Charlie Lee (-62'), Aaron McLean, George Boyd, Dean Keates, Craig Mackail-Smith, Tommy Williams, Sergio Torres (-62'), Gabriel Zakuani

Subs: Chris Westwood, James McKeown, Paul Coutts, Shaun Batt (+62'), Andrew Crofts (+62')

**Colchester United:** Dean Gerken, John White (-34′), Johnnie Jackson, Dean Hammond, Clive Platt, Kem ?zzet, Mark Yeates, Pat Baldwin, Matt Heath (-20′), David Perkins, Jermaine Easter
Subs: Philip Ifil (+20′), Mark Cousins, Scott Vernon, Lee Hills (+34′) (-66′), Anthony Wordsworth (+66′)

Cold up north so a shovel, blanket and Kendall mint cake are packed for the journey. An early escape from work and then through Yeovil with my Posh scarf flying in the wind as a reminder of our recent win. Tedious journey, with an hour plane spotting around Heathrow. Arrive at parents in time for curry, beer and bed.

Saturday dawns; breakfast, read of the local papers. Mid morning sausage rolls to build up our fat reserves as the temperature keeps on dropping. Take a quick look at Sky Sports: "too much Premier League, what about real teams" says dad. Remind him it's the way Posh are heading before we make short work of our pre–match steak pie.

Up the A1 and past Hampton with the old brick chimneys long gone before arriving at London Road. Walked this way so many times and we chat about our memories. Early days in the main stand looking across to the Glebe with families sat on the roof of their houses trying to catch a glimpse of the Posh. Graduating into the London Road End and on a special night in 1974 three generations of us watched Posh win the Div 4 championship. Taking my son along for his first game in the old Glebe Rd and it's here we return. Sampled the Posh catering and dad is not impressed by his £1.50 cup of warm flavoured water.

Old boys Terry Bly and Tony Adcock take to the field to deserved applause. We finalise our plans for the new stadium settling on a double tier London Road, seats in the

Moy's and more tea in the hot water. Must write to Darragh.

Early exchanges see nothing between the sides, game scrappy with the ball disappearing out of play often. Posh show glimpses of class with Williams finding space on the left and Boyd putting through some probing passes. Colchester with a bulked up Platt work hard but no end product. Lewis looks more confident each game. Keates in midfield is breaking up play and Boyd looks to provide a spark. Constant running but no luck for the Mac attack. Colchester are forced into two early substitutions. Half time approaches and many in the packed South Stand make their move towards the tea bar. Old sweats know better. Boyd pushes a ball through to Mackail–Smith, a flick 'a la Paul Gascoigne' over the defender and a half volley into the back of the net.

Posh struggle to get anything going but never look under any threat. 15 mins in and Colchester cross into our box. Platt rises to head home and you just knew it would be him. Suddenly Posh go up a gear and push forward. Two minutes later a cross from the right deep to the back post Zakuani heads back towards goal and the ball is hacked away for Boyd to crack home. More chances come our way: Batt put through by McLean but can't kill the game off. Colchester work hard but Zakuani is pure class as he reads the game well and always has time – this guy is awesome and is our MoM.

Posh won ugly but we had more class and raised our game when needed. Great work ethic, no panic, just hard graft and a willingness to track back, get bodies behind the ball and fight for everything to grind out the win.

Home for a Chinese and a couple of glasses of red. Sunday morning it's snowing! Time to hit the road back to sunny Devon...Posh scarf flying, sunglasses on and a smile on my face. A 445 mile round trip but it's great to be Posh.

*John Middleton*

* * * * *

**25/11/08**

## Swindon Town 2 - 2 Peterborough United

| | |
|---|---|
| Smith '10 | McGovern '20 (o.g.) |
| Cox '81 | Batt '90 |

Att: 6,616

**Swindon Town:** Phil Smith, Jack Smith, Michael Timlin, Hasney Aljofree, Jon-Paul McGovern, Anthony McNamee, Pat Kanyuka, Michael Pook, Billy Paynter (-61'), Simon Cox, Lee Peacock
Subs: Jerel Ifil, Craig Easton, Peter Brezovan, Lilian Nalis (+61'), Ben Joyce
**Peterborough United:** Joe Lewis, Russell Martin, Craig Morgan, Aaron McLean, George Boyd, Dean Keates, Craig Mackail-Smith, Tommy Williams, Sergio Torres (61'), Gabriel Zakuani (-11'), Andrew Crofts
Subs: Chris Westwood (+11'), Charlie Lee, James McKeown, Paul Coutts, Shaun Batt (+61')

Supporting the Posh away is a fantastic experience: you wake up with the buzz of the game in your blood, the thrill of knowing that in just a few hours you will be stood, pint in hand chatting to your friends about everything and anything Posh related and the game that's about to come.

I have been privileged enough to attend some amazing days that make the hair on the back of your neck stand on end and truly make you proud to be a Poshie. Notts County away, when we packed the away stand to the rafters with Poshie's in pink hats chanting and singing as though their lives depended on it, Cobblers at sickfields on New Year's Eve 2005 when a sell-out away stand roared the boys home to a fine one nil win with Chris Plummer grabbing the only goal of the game.

There are also those away trips that make you question your sanity, a Tuesday night in December to Swansea joined by only 33 other hardy souls for example. I had a feeling that the Tuesday night game against Swindon was to be another such night. Had this been a couple of years ago I would have fully expecteded a smattering of away fans on a bloody cold night, at a ground where we haven't always been at our best. However, following Posh is a far different proposition these days and the news that on loan centre back Gabby Zakuani was to sign permanently reminded me just how lucky we are to have a chairman like Darragh.

I set off after work thoroughly expecting that the unbeaten run in the league stretching back to the thrilling 5-4 win against Bristol Rovers would continue. After a quick drive over the bridge from Cardiff I picked up a couple of fellow Poshies and made my way to the Merlin, a pub close to the ground. The pub was as raucous as ever and we even spotted a couple of players' wives. One quick IPA later and we made our way to the County Ground, collected the obligatory pie and hot drink and stepped out into the biting Wiltshire air to be greeted by a few hundred other Posh fans that had made the long journey.

The game got off to a good enough start with Posh enjoying the better of the opening five minutes. Unfortunately disaster struck in the 7th minute when

Zakuani took a shove from behind whilst shepherding the ball out. He fell awkwardly into the gravel surrounding the pitch and remained in a crumpled heap behind the goal. To compound matters with Gabby still receiving treatment behind the goal and Westwood waiting to come on, Jack Smith ran onto a hopeful punt forwards into the gap left behind by the injured player and poked the ball past Lewis.

Posh's equaliser came following good work between Keates and Boyd down the left resulting in the whipped in cross being turned into his own net by a Swindon defender. We were a bit out of sorts throughout the game, lacking a killer final ball or any real build up play. The only half chances landed at the feet of Mackail-Smith and McLean who were unable to convert, even George Boyd was struggling to keep the ball at his feet.

The game appeared to be heading towards a relatively dour stalemate until a spell of pinball in our area resulted in the ball falling to the unmarked Simon Cox who had enough time to finish smartly into the bottom corner of the net. Fortunately for Swindon the linesman failed to notice that he was yards offside.

With only nine minutes left to play I have to confess I thought that was it. Star centre back out injured for however long, the end of the unbeaten run caused by an offside goal and to make matters worse the pie was awful! This however is no ordinary football team. Irrespective of the odds they face they never say die and deep in to injury time Shaun Batt equalised with a wonder strike, a half volley from the top left of the area into the far right corner of the goal. The goal itself was worth the price of admission irrespective of the rest of the game and reminded me exactly how fortunate we are to be watching a team that are very special indeed.

Following the final whistle I bumped into the ever cheerful chairman of PISA, Adi Mowles, and asked what he thought of that? "Shit", was Adi's curt response. Of course he was right, the performance as a whole was not good enough, but the fact that we had played poorly by our own exemplary standards and still come away with a point reminded me that to follow the Posh across the county is never knowing you are beaten.

So remember that whatever the circumstances, whatever the score, the team don't know its over until the final whistle blows. So sing it loud and sing it proud wherever we go: It's Posh we are and Posh we feel, united we all stand, we're telling you, support the blues, the best team in the land!

*Barry Ross*

* * * * *

**25/11/08**

Gabriel Zakuani agrees a three-and-a-half year deal and will join the club on a permanent basis once the January transfer window opens.

* * * * *

**29/11/08**

Prior to the FA Cup Second Round tie with Tranmere Rovers, striker Craig Mackail-Smith was presented with a plaque from club statistician Mick Robinson on behalf of Foreverposh, The Posh Supporters' Trust and PISA 2000. Craig scored Peterborough United's 500th FA Cup goal in the match at AFC Hornchurch.

FA Cup, Second Round

## Peterborough United 0 - 0 Tranmere Rovers

Att: 5,980.

**Peterborough United:** Joe Lewis, Russell Martin, Craig Morgan, Charlie Lee (-46'), Aaron McLean, George Boyd, Dean Keates, Craig Mackail-Smith, Paul Coutts, Tommy Williams, Gabriel Zakuani
Subs: Chris Westwood, James McKeown, Chris Whelpdale, Sergio Torres, Shaun Batt (+46'), Dominic Green, Danny Blanchett
**Tranmere Rovers:** Danny Coyne, Andy Taylor, Ben Chorley, Ian Goodison, Antony Kay, Bas Savage, Ian Moore, Stephen Jennings, Gareth Edds (-71'), Edrissa Sonko, Ryan Shotton
Subs: Godwin Antwi, Terry Gornell (+71'), Luke Waterfall, Aaron Cresswell, Charlie Barnett, Paul Henry, John Achterberg

Oh joy. Tranmere on a Tuesday night for the replay. The incentive to win is an FA Cup third round trip to West Brom. While once more it was pleasing to see Posh prove impossible to break down - largely thanks to the talents of Joe Lewis - it was concerning to see a lack of activity at the business end of the pitch. McLean, Mackail-Smith and Boyd may all work hard and show the odd glimpse of magic, but none are playing to anywhere near the heights we all know they are capable of. Another worry for some fans is the lack of depth in the squad - especially up front and in the middle of the park, more so now that Micah Hyde has had his contract cancelled. One can only assume his rapid fall from club captain to car boot sale-fodder is due to a need to balance the wage budget when Gaby Zakuani signs permanently in January. In other news, Fergie's been shortlisted for November Manager of the Month, the club shop's got some woolly hats in and Tommy's bird is still in the jungle with Mr Sulu and that bloke out of Dollar.

*LondonRoad.net*

*"We worked hard on a change of system through the week, but it didn't work as well as I expected and I need to look at myself a bit for that. Tranmere played very well and if I'm honest the game could have been won by half-time. They deserved to win as we just didn't perform at all so we are very lucky to still be in the competition."*

*Darren Ferguson*

*"It would have been a travesty had Posh found a winning goal."*

*Alan Swann*
*Evening Telegraph*

* * * * *

**30/11/08**

| | | P | W | D | L | Pts |
|---|---|---|---|---|---|---|
| 1 | Leicester | 18 | 11 | 5 | 2 | 38 |
| 2 | MK Dons | 18 | 12 | 1 | 5 | 37 |
| | | | | | | |
| 5 | Posh | 18 | 9 | 6 | 3 | 33 |

# *December*

**06/12/08**

## Stockport County 1 - 3 Peterborough United

Pilkington '52 — Raynes '22 (o.g.), Mackail-Smith '62, Tunnicliffe '75 (o.g.)

Att: 6,148.

**Stockport County:** Owain Fôn Williams, John Mullins (-46'), Dominic Blizzard, Jimmy McNulty, Anthony Pilkington, Gary Dicker (-46'), Tommy Rowe, Michael Raynes (-77'), Stephen Gleeson, Leon McSweeney, Craig Davies
Subs: Michael Rose (+46'), Peter Thompson, Carl Baker, Jason Taylor (+77'), James Tunnicliffe (+46')
**Peterborough United:** Joe Lewis, Russell Martin (-65'), Craig Morgan, Aaron McLean, George Boyd (-89'), Dean Keates, Craig Mackail-Smith, Tommy Williams, Shaun Batt, Gabriel Zakuani, Andrew Crofts
Subs: Chris Westwood, Charlie Lee (+65'), James McKeown, Paul Coutts, Dominic Green (+89')

OK, I admit it. I can't remember the last away game I went to. So why chose to go to a freezing cold Stockport in December? It's a long story involving wives, daughters, stepsons and Christmas shopping but, you're right, you don't want to know. You want to know about the game. Quite right too. It was good and we won. The End.

More detail? Well, you see, it was my wife and daughter and Dave's wife who wanted to go shopping so we went to Pudsey by car, used my bus pass to get into Leeds, used my railcard to get to Manchester, got rid of the women for shopping and then took the train to Stockport. We were to meet Dave's mates in the Grapes but he didn't know where it was so we took a taxi. We now know it's 200 yards from the station. Decent pub but be wary of the Old Tom which is 8.5% ABV and brewed by Robinsons in Stockport. This could account for you missing the match.

Posh started much the brighter of the sides on a pitch which still showed the markings, and damage, from the previous night's rugby. Aaron McLean had two good early strikes well saved by the curiously named Fon Williams. Welsh, I suppose.

Stockport slowly improved and began to knock the ball about a bit. I've never seen a better team at passing the ball square seventeen times. Unfortunately for them such moves generally foundered on a solid Peterborough defence and Joe Lewis' only problem was how to keep warm. In contrast, Craig Mackail-Smith was a real thorn in the opposition's side, covering a lot of ground and causing panic whenever he had the ball. McLean too, was difficult to handle and it was his persistence which led to the first goal as his low cross was sliced past Fon Williams by Raynes. Posh continued to dominate and the goalkeeper had to be sharp to push away Batt's effort towards the end of the half.

I ordered a large sausage roll and covered myself in the piping hot flaky pastry in an attempt to warm up. Lovely. Dave had a cheese and onion pie as he's a veggie and a

Posh supporter. And my stepson. He's got problems that boy.

After the break, Stockport came out fighting. They were quickly rewarded with one of those moments which happen but seldom in a player's career. The ball broke to Pilkington on the left and he turned and lashed in a shot which somehow found the gap between Joe Lewis' outstretched hand and the inside of the post. 1-1.

This awoke the slumbering Stockport fans who gave vocal encouragement to their side for the first time and, for a few minutes, Posh were swaying slightly if not quite rocking. However, prompted by George Boyd, Posh soon regained the upper hand and Fon Williams was twice lucky to have shots directed straight at him. He could do nothing when Boyd took advantage of a defensive mix up to cross for Mackail-Smith to score Posh's thoroughly deserved second. Stockport lapsed back into mediocrity and with 15 minutes left the game was out of their reach when another cross from Batt was deflected into his own net by Tunnicliffe, who probably wished he'd stayed on the bench.

There was no question of Posh hanging on to the lead though and the visitor's best move of the game saw Boyd's shot crash against the underside of the bar and rebound to safety - scant reward for his endeavour. He and Batt had been booked earlier for late challenges as my shouts of "Don't commit yourself" went unheeded. Hey, ho!

Many Stockport fans had already left the ground before the final whistle but we caught up with a few of them in the Grapes afterwards. They had the grace to admit our forwards had been too hot for them but, for some unfathomable reason, they didn't think our defence was any good!. Well, I guess they had to console themselves somehow. I think they were on the Old Tom.

* * * * *

**09/12/08**

FA Cup Second Round Replay

Tranmere Rovers 1 - 2 Peterborough United

Kay '47 McLean '90

Mackail-Smith '114

Att: 3,139 (159 away).

**Tranmere Rovers:** Danny Coyne, Godwin Antwi, Andy Taylor, Ben Chorley, Ian Goodison, Antony Kay, Bas Savage, Ian Moore (-93'), Stephen Jennings, Gareth Edds (-62'), Edrissa Sonko (-88')
Subs: Terry Gornell (+93'), Luke Waterfall, Aaron Cresswell (+88'), Charlie Barnett, Paul Henry, Chris Shuker (+62'), John Achterberg
**Peterborough United:** Joe Lewis, Craig Morgan, Charlie Lee, Aaron McLean, George Boyd, Dean Keates, Craig Mackail-Smith, Paul Coutts, Shaun Batt (-75'), Gabriel Zakuani (-91'), Danny Blanchett (-83')
Subs: Chris Westwood (+91'), James McKeown, Chris Whelpdale (+83'), Sergio Torres, Dominic Green (+75'), Lewis Webb, Sam Gaughran

A Cup replay in Birkenhead on a Tuesday night is hardly anyone's idea of a good time. However, after drawing with Tranmere at London Road I decided I would go to this one to tick off a new ground and hopefully see us win and go on to get a big side in the third round. I had a look at train times and prices but didn't fancy spending six hours in Chester station on the way home, so managed to arrange a lift.

I managed to get in a couple of lessons at college before heading to Peterborough station to hitch a ride up to

Tranmere. In anticipation of the gruelling trip ahead someone had come prepared to educate me with a DVD of the 1992 Wembley win against Stockport. The journey was as good as a three-hour car journey can get.

Once in Tranmere we found the best spot to park was slap bang in between the pub and the ground. The carvery at the pub was only £4 and went down a treat with a couple of beers. Then after a chin wag with a few other fans I wandered out and queued at the ticket office to get my 'tax dodger' ticket only to find I could've paid cash on the turnstiles. Got in and parked my bum on a seat towards the back and was quite impressed with the ground, although the temperature must have been below zero - I was freezing. The temperature continued to drop and the standard of football was hardly brilliant. At half-time I went downstairs into the concourse for a bit of warmth.

Shortly after the restart Tranmere grabbed a goal and the game got a bit more entertaining. Both sides pressed to no avail and we were getting ready to up and leave when, in the last minute, Aaron McLean scored a real poachers goal. It sent us crazy and I hadn't travelled for nothing. On the other hand we also realised we were out in the cold for at least another 30 mins (as did the stewards, two of whom were none too pleased.)

Posh livened up the tempo of the game and Craig Mackail Smith put us into the lead. It was brilliant, the locals who had been taunting us 20 mins earlier were now leaving the stadium. It was a complete role reversal and we loved it. Posh pressed for a third and hit the post but the real relief came when the ref blew for the end of the game.

The win made the journey home a lot more pleasant than it would have been had we lost. I was in bed at about 3am. Many would disagree with me but I thought - 'what a good day.'

*Glen Townsend*

*"This team just don't know when they are beaten. They kept going, they never gave up and showed great character and determination. I think on the night we deserved to progress, we hit the woodwork four times and I think after they scored, we dominated for long spells."*

*Darren Ferguson*

* * * * *

**13/12/08**

## Peterborough United 2 - 2 Oldham Athletic

McLean '12 Hughes '40
McLean '37 Hughes '59

Att: 6,219 (481 away).

**Peterborough United:** Joe Lewis,Russell Martin, Craig Morgan, Aaron McLean, George Boyd, Dean Keates, Craig Mackail-Smith, Tommy Williams (-46'), Shaun Batt (-65'), Gabriel Zakuani, Andrew Crofts
Subs: Chris Westwood, Charlie Lee (+46'), James McKeown, Paul Coutts, Dominic Green (+65')
**Oldham Athletic:** Greg Fleming, Neil Eardley, Stefan Stam, Danny Whitaker, Mark Allott, Lee Hughes, Kelvin Lomax, Reuben Hazell, Chris Taylor, Daniel Jones (-30'), Darren Byfield
Subs: Chris O'Grady, Kevin Maher, Kieran Lee, Andy Liddell (+30'), Lewis Alessandra

For a lot of Posh fans the home game experience lasts for about three hours. Leave the house around 2.15, into the ground for 2.45, watch the Posh (usually win) and then off home for around 5.30. Some extend this by going for a beverage or three before the game. I have recently read a surprising statistic that 60% of Posh fans don't live within the Peterborough area. I am one of this 60%. Not only do I live 30 miles away I also play football for PUSFC. That's the Peterborough United Supporters Football Club and we play against supporters of other football clubs - generally that days opposition - on the morning before a game.

Arriving at Bushfield Leisure Centre in the cold, wind and rain we get changed to discover we only have 11 players. Enough for a team, I agree, but at my age we really do need some subs to cover. The game goes well and we win 4-0 against a surprisingly good-natured side. I hate to think what time they set out to get here. Afterwards I head to Ebenezers for a quick drink and a chat with friends. We all agree Oldham will be hard to beat but we think we will just edge it. General concensus is a 2-1 Posh win.

Posh start much brighter than Oldham with the challenges flying in. McLean gets booked inside the first ten mins followed by Whitaker. McLean scores after twelve mins with a very big deflection that loops over the goalkeeper. Then the first contentious decision by the inept referee – he awards a penalty as McLean appears to be brought down by the goalkeeper. If he thinks it's a penalty then surely the keeper must be off? Nope, he gives a yellow. McLean steps up and the keeper saves.

Morgan gets booked for a poor challenge on Jones who gets carried off on a stretcher. All of this inside twenty five mins. Ten minutes later MacKail-Smith gets pushed as he's about to score from a yard out and the ref gives another penalty. Surely this one warrants a red card? Apparently not. This time MacKail-Smith steps up to take the penalty but he manages to hit the post. Fortunately McLean is the first to react and scores with the rebound to make it 2-0. Just as we think we're coasting to a comfortable half-time lead we concede a corner. Lewis half clears the cross and it falls to Lee Hughes who chips it over everybody to end the half at 2-1.

At half time Tom Williams is replaced by Charlie Lee. Both teams attack with Russ Martin and McLean both having shots stopped and Lewis pulling off a fantastic save at the other end. Oldham score from a well worked free kick although Lewis should not have dropped the initial shot from Liddell allowing Hughes to tap in from three yards out. As Posh start to fade Hughes picks up a booking for a foul on Lee much to the amusement of the crowd. Dominic Green replaces Batt and he supplies McLean for Posh's best chance of the second half. Oldham almost steal it in the dying minutes but somehow Zakuani manages to head over the bar.

An eventful game with seven yellow cards, four goals, two penalties and no sending offs. As I set off in my car I listen to Radio Cambridgeshire and disagree with most of the people who have rung and texted in their opinions of the game. My day with Posh will last the usual nine hours.

*Andy Mills*

Almost 80 years to the day, in a small terraced house on the outskirts of Oldham, Bernard Cribbins was born. Famous for narrating The Wombles, Cribbins would have been amused to see the rubbish on display at London Road today. Posh have a reputation now for making good use of the things that we find, and on 12 mins a McLean cross found and made good use of opposition defender Stefan Stam, who put the ball in his own net to leave Oldham behind. Posh were then given two penalties, the first taken by McLean was saved then Mackail-Smith took the second, hitting the post before McLean slotted home the rebound. Lee Hughes has previously spent three years in prison, dreaming of wombling free, and it was he that scored twice to level the match. After 70 mins or so Shaun Batt, son of the legendary Mike Batt, was replaced by Green who later on cleared the ball off the line to prevent Oldham winning it at the death. The game disappointingly finished at 2-2, although even more disappointing was my inability to find puns or analogies for Tobermory, Orinoco and Madame Cholet. Anyway, I hope you all have a Wombling Merry Christmas.

*LondonRoad.net*

* * * * *

**20/12/08**

## Leicester City 4 - 0 Peterborough United

Morgan '6 (o.g.)
Fryatt '38
King '70
Howard '90

Att: 23,390.

**Leicester City:** David Martin, Kerrea Gilbert, Aleksandur Tunchev, Matthew Oakley, Steve Howard, Lloyd Dyer, Matty Fryatt (-72′), Andy King, Jack Hobbs, Bruno Berner, Mark Davies
Subs: Michael Morrison, Max Gradel, Paul Dickov (+72′), Chris Powell, Alex Cisak
**Peterborough United:** Joe Lewis, Russell Martin, Craig Morgan, Chris Westwood (-46′), Charlie Lee, Aaron McLean, George Boyd, Dean Keates, Craig Mackail-Smith (-76′), Chris Whelpdale, Andrew Crofts (-76′)
Subs: James McKeown, Paul Coutts (+46′), Shaun Batt (+76′), Dominic Green (+76′), Danny Blanchett

The plan was a simple one. Celebrate Christmas with three colleagues by taking in the Leicester game and then having a curry. The fact that one of those colleagues, Matt, is a Leicester fan, added a little more spice to the whole football/curry combo.

I was driving (rather than face a train nightmare) so picked up fellow Fen-dwellers Mike and Trev (neutrals for today) and set off for Leicester's glitzy Belgrave Road, where we would abandon the car in a side-street and wander off to find Matt among the odd Hobbit-like creatures that seem to inhabit this crumbling East Midlands city. Seriously, a walk through the city centre made me feel like a giant. A handsome giant. A handsome giant with no form of palsy. To the casual observer it must have been like watching Brad Pitt on stilts, striding his way through a Danny Devito cloning experiment gone horribly wrong.

After rescuing Matt from Lilliput Bus Station, we made our way to the ground. Matt and Mike had tickets to sit with the Leicester lot, while me and Trev were in with the Poshies. Our stop at a pub to break up the two-and-a-half-mile walk had meant we didn't have a lot of time to spare before kick-off. Just enough time to stick a quid on 2-0, CMS first scorer, and to experience the most slippery floor ever created by man. The concourse of the away fans block at the Walkers had been kindly transformed into Poshies on Ice by the helpful Foxes ground staff.

Having done our best Torvill and Dean impression, we took to our seats and within six minutes of the game kicking off it was clear that this was not to be a our day. Craig Morgan's absurdly sliced own goal was followed by three more bulges of Joe's net. Let's just say that's about as much as I can bring myself to say about the match itself.

I had more important things to worry about. Chiefly, meeting up with Foxes fan Matt and facing a 45-minute walk to the curry house packed with gloating.

In fairness to the man, he greeted me only with a huge smile and a shake of the head. I waited for the spring in his step to carry him on ahead of us, before unleashing a full ball-by-ball analysis on Mike, who, having listened to me bigging up Boyd, CMS and co, wondered if he'd been watching the right team.

Thankfully, the food at Bobby's on Belgrave Road was simply magical - tastier than Charlie Lee in a bare-knuckle fight, crisper than an Aaron McLean snapshot and hotter than George Boyd in a leopard-print thong.

www.eatatbobbys.com

*Jack Thorpe*

*"I really feel for the supporters. I stressed before the game that this was an important fixture for the fans, they haven't sampled a fixture with Leicester for a while and it was a*

*big day out for them. They were fantastic, they came in their numbers and it is really disappointing that we couldn't give them anything to cheer about,"*

*Darren Ferguson*

* * * * *

**26/12/08**

## Peterborough United 1 - 0 Millwall
McLean '23

Att: 9,351 (1,564 away).

**Peterborough United:** Joe Lewis, Russell Martin, Craig Morgan, Charlie Lee, Aaron McLean, George Boyd (-81'), Dean Keates, Craig Mackail-Smith, Paul Coutts (-89'), Chris Whelpdale (-73'), Tommy Williams
Subs: Chris Westwood, Shaun Batt (+73'), Dominic Green (+81'), Andrew Crofts (+89'), Danny Blanchett
**Millwall:** David Forde, Paul Robinson, Zak Whitbread, Alan Dunne, Gary Alexander, Lewis Grabban (-35'), Tony Craig (-31'), Trésor Kandol (-67'), Ashley Grimes (-58'), Nadjim Abdou, Adam Bolder
Subs: Neil Harris (+67'), Scott Barron (+35'), Dave Martin (+58'), Marc Laird, Lenny Pidgeley

For me, a trip to London Road is a rare occurrence these days. I now live 5000 miles away in Texas so the trips home limit me to two or three games per season. My last visit coincided with a 2-1 home defeat to Hartlepool.

It is then typical that Posh would go on to a long unbeaten run as soon as I cleared off back to Dallas. Of course, the day I step foot back into this country the unbeaten run comes to an end with a 4-0 defeat at Leicester. Coincidence? Probably, but seeing as how my luggage failed to arrive on the same plane as I did maybe this trip was doomed before it began.

The last time I had seen Posh play Millwall was at the New Den when Jason Lee and Andy Clarke were sent off by referee Phil Pr(T)osser and 'We only needed 9 men'. I expected that the atmosphere at London Road would be a little more welcoming than that day in March 2001. Once you add Posh's Boxing Day history to the jinx I seem to have on the team, I suddenly was not so optimistic about our chances against Millwall. However from most reports I have had, the football we have been playing is far above what has been seen in recent years. So it was with much interest that I made my way to London Road on Boxing Day.

A noon kick-off saw to it that my daughter Gemma and I set off about 10am for the usual pre-match beer and banter in Ebs. We made a quick stop at the club shop to exchange my daughter's new Posh shirt for one of the right size and managed to bump into Aaron McLean. Aaron graciously signed her shirt and accepted our thanks and good luck wishes. At Eb's we were greeted by some of the familiar faces that keep PISA 2000 on it's feet.

After being one of the founding members of PISA 2000 it makes me proud to know that the organisation has been able to evolve through its committee and members to be the organisation that it is today. Regular meetings with the club mean that the voices of the members are heard whether they are positive or negative. Obviously Darragh MacAnthony also needs much of the credit too as the conversation is two way. PISA 2000 also holds such events as the Legends Evening and coach trips to certain away games. Anyway onto the game at hand.

A healthy looking crowd was already in place by the time we took our seats. Posh played particularly well in the first half and took the lead through MacLean. Millwall showed their quality at times but were down to 10 men with the sending off of Tony Craig for an elbow to Whelpdale's head. The second half saw Millwall take control of the game, but they could not break through and get the equalizer. So Posh break the voodoo, the jinx, the hex or even the curse. Whatever it was it is broken and a valuable three points are won in front of over 9000 fans.

This was likely to be my last visit of this season so it was great to see a victory. As someone who can't get to many games I would advise anyone to get to as many games as possible. Great things are happening to our team.

*Nigel Curtis*

* * * * *

**28/12/08**

## Cheltenham Town 3 - 6 Peterborough United

| | |
|---|---|
| Vincent '48 (pen.) | Boyd '3 |
| Hammond '67 | Lee '60 |
| Owusu '86 | Mackail-Smith '63 |
| | Wright '75 (o.g.) |
| | McLean '87 |
| | Whelpdale '90 |

Att: 3,976 (504 away).

**Cheltenham Town:** Scott Brown, Alan Wright, Josh Low, Alex Russell, Ashley Vincent, Lee Ridley, Gallinagh (-71'), Barry Hayles (-89'), Darren Kenton, Ian Westlake, Elvis Hammond (-89')

Subs: Paul Connor, Andy Lindegaard, Will Puddy, Jonathan Hayes (+89'), Lloyd Owusu (+71')
**Peterborough United:** Joe Lewis, Russell Martin, Craig Morgan, Charlie Lee, Aaron McLean, George Boyd, Dean Keates, Craig Mackail-Smith, Paul Coutts (-85'), Chris Whelpdale, Tommy Williams
Subs: Chris Westwood, Shaun Batt, Dominic Green, Andrew Crofts (+85'), Danny Blanchett

My last game before heading back to Italy after seeing us get hammered at Leicester and beating Millwall. So it's Cheltenham here I come Also a special day out as it's my best mate MP's birthday We all met at mine at 10 and I said I would drive so Marco could have a drink.

Arrived with plenty of time to spare and found a pub near the ground but it looked a bit rough but we decided to risk it. Good decision as the Sunday roast was amazing. We got to the Ground and thought there would only be a handfull of supporters but it was full. Great turn out and great vocal support.

We started well and scored early on but we should've had a couple more. The second half was mad. It went something like 1-1 1-2 1-3 2-3 2-4 3-4 3-5 and then 3-6. Amazing. This being my last game before going back to Italy I couldn't have asked for a better farewell.

*Davide Broccoli*

* * * * *

**31/12/08**

| | | P | W | D | L | Pts |
|---|---|---|---|---|---|---|
| 1 | Leicester | 23 | 15 | 6 | 2 | 51 |
| 2 | MK Dons | 23 | 16 | 1 | 6 | 49 |
| | | | | | | |
| 4 | Posh | 23 | 12 | 7 | 4 | 43 |

# January

**03/01/09**

FA Cup Third Round

West Bromwich Albion 1-1 Peterborough Utd

Olsson '64 Mackail-Smith '87

Att: 18,659.

**West Bromwich Albion:** Scott Carson, Carl Hoefkens, Marek Cech, Leon Barnett, Robert Koren (-46'), Jonathan Greening, Roman Bednár (-76'), Chris Brunt, Luke Moore (-70'), Jonas Olsson, Borja Valero
Subs: Dean Kiely, Paul Robinson, Craig Beattie (+76'), Kim Do-Heon, Graham Dorrans (+70'), Jay Simpson (+46'), Ryan Donk
**Peterborough United:** Joe Lewis, Russell Martin, Craig Morgan, Charlie Lee, Aaron McLean (-89'), George Boyd, Dean Keates, Craig Mackail-Smith, Paul Coutts, Chris Whelpdale (-75'), Gabriel Zakuani
Subs: Chris Westwood, James McKeown, Sergio Torres (+89'), Shaun Batt (+75'), Dominic Green, Danny Andrew, Danny Blanchett

FA Cup third round, where all men are equal and so it was. Uneventful journey up from Devon arriving at the Premier Inn at midday, pity we were booked into the Travelodge.

Walking through an area resembling Beirut in the early 80s we marched past the Hawthorns to the less than magnificent Royal Oak. It was packed out by the blue army – a couple of pints of Banks' some pre-match banter and a bit of people-watching. Fuelled up, Ben and I made our way to find the Smethwick Rd End already packed. This was going to be a special day.

The teams came out and the Posh fans were in fine voice, real lump in the throat time. Early exchanges saw nothing between the teams. The Baggies took an early grip on the game and Lewis flapped at a corner but the defence held firm. Slowly Posh began to play with Keates' bite and Coutts' passing the midfield began to see more of the ball. Craig Mackail-Smith cuts in from the left and shoots - only to see his effort thump against the bar. Posh force three corners in quick succession and the Baggies are on the back foot. Zakuani superbly defends a Bednar effort and Morgan makes a fantastic tackle on the edge of the area that had the Poshies out of their seats. Charlie Lee was having a blinder and with Martin on the right we were comfortable. Half time 0–0.

Time to check out the bogs, with only one door in/out you didn't want to be desperate. Posh attacked the away end and it was time to savour our talented strike force. The game opens up with Boyd finding space on the left and CMS worrying the opposition back four with relentless running. The Baggies were losing it both on and off the pitch as the Posh supporters grew louder. Against the run of play and from a corner up pops Olsson to head home. The Boro boys (and girls) make even more noise.

A shot by Boyd hits the stanchion. Another cross from Boyd and CMS heads wide. More chances fall to McLean and CMS but they fail to convert. We were battering them with Boyd on the ball, beats three, goes down but gets the pass away. Posh support now trying to will the ball into the net and we thought we had done it as George Boyd scores but is judged offside.

Batt outside the area, ball to McLean, low cross into the 6 yd box. Touch by CMS – you beauty!! 1–1. Massive outpouring of noise and emotion hits us all. Posh look for the winner and a McLean effort at the end just goes wide. Home fans rush away at the final whistle whilst we celebrate. To a man we were equal and we never gave up. A year ago the Baggies played us off the park but today shows how far we have come in such a short time.

Out of the ground and back to The Royal Oak for a few pints and then back to Travelodge. Time for a famous Midlands curry but we shouldn't have bothered as Oldbury was boarded up, shut or demolished. So we settled for a kebab, a few cans and watched the highlights on TV. Slept well and we were so proud to be Posh.

*John Middleton*

* * * * *

**05/01/09**

Chris Westwood joins Cheltenham Town on a one-month loan deal.

* * * * *

**06/01/09**

The game against MK Dons is postponed due to a frozen pitch.

* * * * *

**08/01/09**

Scott Rendell's loan move to Cambridge United hits a snag. I won't bore you with the details but apparently Cambridge director George Rolls didn't turn up with the cash. Maybe he just didn't have a spare envelope or went to a lay-by on the M1 instead of the A1?

* * * * *

**09/01/09**

A second postponement of the week as the clash at Tranmere is called off.

* * * * *

**13/01/09**

FA Cup Second Round Replay

Peterborough Utd 0 - 2 West Bromwich Albion

Simpson '18

Robinson '37

Att: 10,735 (1,459 away).

**Peterborough United:** Joe Lewis, Russell Martin, Craig Morgan, Charlie Lee (-77'), Aaron McLean, George Boyd, Dean Keates, Craig Mackail-Smith, Chris Whelpdale, Tommy Williams, Gabriel Zakuani
Subs: James McKeown, Sergio Torres, Shaun Batt (+77'), Dominic Green, Lewis Webb, Sam Gaughran, Danny Blanchett
**West Bromwich Albion:** Scott Carson, Carl Hoefkens, Paul Robinson, Leon Barnett, Robert Koren, Jonathan Greening, Roman Bednár, Kim Do-Heon (-80'), Filipe Teixeira (-65'), Jay Simpson (-71'), Ryan Donk
Subs: Dean Kiely, Chris Brunt, Craig Beattie (+71'), Luke Moore, Graham Dorrans (+65'), Pedro Pelé, Borja Valero (+80')

The bloke who was supposed to be doing this report couldn't get in the ground. After queuing for 45 mins to get a ticket, he then joined another queue only to be told that the ground was full and that he should've arrived at least two hours before kick-off if he was serious about wanting to watch the match. So he turned around and went home.

He didn't miss much. Posh couldn't sum up the battling magnificence of the draw at the Hawthorns and succumbed rather weakly in front of a big, but not sold out, crowd.

Simpson scored with a long-range effort and Robinson popped up at the back post to nod in a simple header and it was over by half-time. West Brom were comfortable all night and I went home quite annoyed that I'd spent £20 on such a disappointing performance.

*Paul Mitchell*

* * * * *

**17/01/09**

## Peterborough United 1 - 0 Walsall
Whelpdale '6

Att: 5,705 (295 away).

**Peterborough United:** Joe Lewis, Russell Martin, Craig Morgan, Charlie Lee, Aaron McLean, George Boyd, Dean Keates, Craig Mackail-Smith, Paul Coutts, Chris Whelpdale, Gabriel Zakuani
Subs: Scott Rendell, Sergio Torres, Shaun Batt, Andrew Crofts, Danny Blanchett
**Walsall:** Clayton Ince, Anthony Gerrard, Chris Palmer (-23'), Dwayne Mattis, Jabo Ibehre, Mark Bradley, Richard Taundry, Alex Nicholls, Troy Deeney (-72'), Emmanuele Smith,Netan Sansara
Subs: Rene Gilmartin, Marco Reich (+72'), Richard Davies, Sam Adkins (+23'), Hassan Bacchus

*An early goal from Chris Whelpdale gave Posh a comfortable victory over Walsall. Whelpdale prodded the ball past visiting goalkeeper Clayton Ince after a Charlie Lee long throw. Posh controlled most of the match, but found visiting goalkeeper Clayton Ince an enormous obstacle. Ince flew through the air to catch Aaron McLean's spectacular long-range volley, but did even better to keep out George Boyd's close-range strike. Ince also deflected a Boyd shot onto a post and somehow thwarted Craig Mackail-Smith from six yards. Walsall rarely threatened an equaliser.*

*The Evening Telegraph*

*"When I came into the club it was a shambles. Players were eating KFC and getting changed for training and matches in their cars. It has changed so much since I arrived at the club and I honestly don't know what football the supporters were watching two years ago because I am pretty confident it is a lot better now. We are sitting fourth in the division and are within a few points of the automatic promotion places after securing automatic promotion last season. I don't understand why the supporters are moaning about players within my side. We have a young squad and they need the support of the fans. George Boyd is a nervous wreck at the minute because every time he loses the ball the crowd moans and shouts obscenities at him."*

*Darren Ferguson*

* * * * *

**19/01/09**

Scott Rendell rejoins Cambridge United on-loan until the end of the season. Hooray.

* * * * *

**20/01/09**

## Peterborough United 0 - 0 MK Dons

Att: 8,982 (1,108 away).

**Peterborough United:** Joe Lewis, Russell Martin, Craig Morgan, Charlie Lee, Aaron McLean, George Boyd, Dean Keates, Craig Mackail-Smith, Paul Coutts, Chris Whelpdale (-69'), Gabriel Zakuani
Subs: James McKeown, Sergio Torres, Shaun Batt (+69'), Andrew Crofts, Danny Blanchett
**MK Dons:** Willy Guéret, Dean Lewington, Miguel Ángel Llera (-70'), Sean O'Hanlon, Jemal Johnson (-61'), Aaron Wilbraham, Sam Baldock, Shaun Cummings, Alan Navarro, Luke Howell, Peter Leven
Subs: Nathan Abbey, Jude Stirling (+70'), Ali Gerba, Luke Chadwick (+61'), Tore André Flo

We've managed to nab five minutes out of the busy schedule of America's first black president (or 44th white president, depending on how you look at it) to get his insight into tonight's match. Take it away, Barry:

"My fellow Poshies, we stand here today not because we choose to, but because we have to. There is evil in the world - people whose ideals and beliefs seem alien to us. Who seemingly have no morals, no conscience, no sense of shame. I refer, of course, to MK Dons fans. I'm immensely proud and humbled to support the Posh – as a man whose father, less than 10 years ago, would have been refused entry to Stadium MK. Because it didn't exist. Great names, like Lawrie Sanchez, John Fashanu, Robbie Earle - their effort and endeavours removed from our children's history books. And these people, these MK Dons fans are ignorant to it all.

These are the type of people who happily watch a team of men dive, cheat, whine, spoil and stall their way through 90 minutes of football. These are the type of people who think Jude Stirling offers something to their team. These are the type of people who wear baseball caps to a football match. These are the type of people who fly to Spain to spend a week eating at McDonalds and drinking John Smith's Smooth in O'Flaherty's Irish Pub. Yes, they are rising through the divisions, but, my friends, so are we. And we're doing it with style, with flair, with a sense of fair play.

Today I say to you that the challenges we face, in rising above these imposters in the league table, are real. They are serious and they are many. They will not be met easily or in a short span of time. But know this, Posh fans - they will be met. So let us mark this day with remembrance, of who we are and how far we have travelled.

In the year of Big Ron's arrival, in the coldest of months, a small band of Posh fans huddled on desolate terraces. The promotion charge was faltering. Lloyd Opara was our biggest signing. Danny Crow was starting to fill out a bit. At a moment when the outcome of our promotion chase was most in doubt, the leader of our men ordered these words be read to his people: "When it's a battle, you fookin' battle."

Poshies. In the face of our common dangers, in this winter of our hardship, let us remember these timeless words. With hope and virtue, let us brave once more the icy currents, and endure what storms may come. Let it be said by our children's children that when we were tested we refused to let this journey end, that we did not turn back nor did we falter; and with eyes fixed on the horizon and Boyd's grace upon us, we carried forth that great gift of freedom and delivered it safely to future generations.

Thank you. Boyd bless you. And Boyd bless Peterborough United Football Club.

*Barry Obama*

*"And your travelling army of synthetic supporters*
*would be taken away from you and thrown in the bin."*

*Half Man Half Biscuit*

* * * * *

**22/01/09**

Defender Tom Williams undergoes an operation on his knee which will rule him out of action for up to five weeks.

* * * * *

**24/01/09**

Leeds United 3 - 1 Peterborough United

| Leeds United | Peterborough United |
|---|---|
| Beckford '62 | Mackail-Smith '79 |
| Beckford '71 | |
| Howson '90 | |

Att: 22,766.

**Leeds United:** Casper Ankergren, Jonathan Douglas, Rui Marques, Luciano Becchio (-58′), Fabian Delph, Bradley Johnson, Andy Robinson (-88′), Andy Hughes, Lee Trundle (-81′), Richard Naylor, Carl Dickinson
Subs: ?ubomír Michalík, Jermaine Beckford (+58′), David Lucas, Jonny Howson (+81′), Robert Snodgrass (+88′)
**Peterborough United:** Joe Lewis, Russell Martin, Craig Morgan, Charlie Lee, Aaron McLean, George Boyd, Dean Keates, Craig Mackail-Smith, Paul Coutts, Chris Whelpdale (-89′), Gabriel Zakuani
Subs: James McKeown, Sergio Torres, Shaun Batt (+89′), Andrew Crofts, Danny Blanchett

I moved to Leeds on 8 September 1996, the day before Posh drew 1-1 with Wrexham. Leeds were playing Manchester United. Posh finished the season 21st in the division and were relegated to the bottom tier. Leeds were still in the premiership. Such comparisons are tiresome, though we are all well aware of Leeds rapid descent down the divisions, but in this case it is relevant. For most of the 13 years I've lived in Leeds the biggest chance we had of playing Leeds was in the sweaty hands of someone like Peter Beardsley fondling balls in a cloth sack at Soho Square.

There was something great about living in a city that hosted champions league football, the influx of European supporters seemed to make the place more cosmopolitan. Briggate was more like Las Ramblas than the dour tedious shopping street it really is. As good as this was, Leeds in League One is infinitely better. To work amongst the once proud Leeds fans is wonderful, my office is possibly the only one in England where the people won't talk about football, because to talk about football is to acknowledge that Leeds United are practically in the basement of English football.

Most of you, I wager, can get in your car at 2pm and drive to London Road, then within half an hour of leaving the game you'll be home with a cup of tea looking at the results on ceefax. You probably take this for granted, but for exiled fans every game is a military operation. For every game we have to meet at the rendezvous at the agreed time, get the agreed train, meet in the agreed pub and go home on the agreed train. It's meticulously planned so no-one gets lost or turns up late, but it's so frustrating. This time it was going to be different, this time I could go to a game at my own leisure.

At 9am most Posh fans were waiting for the train to Leeds, while I was treating my pregnant wife to the full range of my best snores. I didn't even leave the house until after 2pm, I strolled down Churwell Hill walked across the ring road and within 45 minutes I was hanging around the Billy Bremner statue waiting for Trev to appear with my ticket.

I'd only been to Elland Road once before, I sat in the newish stand right at the top to see England v Australia play rugby (Australia won). I seem to recall the view was amazing, the facilities top notch and the food of a high standard. Either things are different in the away end or my memory is shot to shit, because this time the view was awful, the facilities practically non existent and the food, thankfully, came with a free sick bag.

The problem is that the away fans are stuck in a corner of the ground, so you are too far from the action, unless all the action happens at one corner flag. The upside of this is that all the Posh fans were squashed together and as a result made a lot of noise. It has been a long time since I've experienced such a good atmosphere with Posh, we were able to generate a lot of noise in what is still Englands 11th largest football stadium. The kind of stadium that if Darragh has his way, we'll be playing in week in week out.

If Posh were over-awed by the size of the ground they certainly didn't show it, Posh controlled the game in the first half but sadly were unable to take the lead. In the second half we continued to dominate until Leeds were gifted a dodgy free kick, then as if that wasn't enough the ball spilled out of Lewis's hands into the path of a grateful Jermaine Beckford. This was the turning point, suddenly Leeds looked like the Leeds of old and within 10 mins made it 2-0. The Posh fans did not lose faith though, despite being 2-0 down we continued to spur on the team, who responded by taking control of the game again. Two excellent attacks were thwarted before Mackail-Smith pulled one back. Posh were back in contention, "We could win this", I said, but I was wrong. As Posh threw everything into getting an equaliser Leeds caught us on the break and finished the game off. An underserving end to a good Posh performance.

I walked home dejected, I've been waiting so long to see Posh at Elland Road, I hadn't considered what would happen if we lost. On Monday it will be me avoiding the subject of football whilst the Leeds fans will be laughing like the braying wankers they are.

*Andy Gardner*

* * * * *

**25/01/09**

*"The chairman has offered me about five players in the last week and one player alone would have cost around £400,000, but I am happy with the squad I have. If I was to bring anyone in they would have to have the right temperament and also fit in with the dressing room. The team spirit this side have is fantastic and they would have to be really good players to get into this team. I don't envisage any players coming in before the end of the January transfer window and I am certainly pleased with the personnel that I have in the squad."*

*Darren Ferguson*

* * * * *

**27/01/09**

Peterborough United 4 - 2 Crewe Alexandra

| | |
|---|---|
| Boyd '50 | Pope '2 |
| McLean '53 | Pope '57 |
| Keates '69 | |
| Boyd '87 | |

Att: 5,775 (119 away).

**Peterborough United:** Joe Lewis, Russell Martin, Charlie Lee, Aaron McLean, George Boyd, Dean Keates (-89'), Craig Mackail-Smith (-89'), Paul Coutts, Chris Whelpdale (-66'), Gabriel Zakuani, Danny Blanchett
Subs: Sergio Torres, Shaun Batt (+66'), Dominic Green (+89'), Andrew Crofts (+89'), Sam Gaughran
**Crewe Alexandra:** Stuart Tomlinson, Danny Woodards, Billy Jones, Mark Carrington, Tom Pope (-89'), Colin Daniel (-75'), Clayton Donaldson, John Brayford, Dennis Lawrence, Danny Shelley (-73'), Marlon Broomes
Subs: Steve Collis, Calvin Zola (+89'), Joel Grant (+75'), George Abbey, Shaun Miller (+73')

*It has been suggested recently that George Boyd might be lacking in self-confidence. If so, Piers Morgan is modest rather than smug, Craig Bellamy is loyal and Steve McClaren is a tactical genius.*

*Boyd probably hasn't been nervous since his last school exam. He's so laid-back he should carry a sun lounger strapped to his back, but when you possess his amount of natural ability, football should never cause you a moment's worry.*

*Boyd teased and tormented Crewe last night to pull Posh back from the possibility of an embarrassing result against League One's bottom club. Two goals, both struck with his weaker right foot, helped turn a 1-0 half-time deficit into a 4-2 win in a match that was never comfortable for the rest of those with Posh blood.*

*Alan Swann*
*The Evening Telegraph*

* * * * *

**31/01/09**

## Huddersfield Town 1 - 0 Peterborough United

Collins '35

Att: 14,480 (642 away)

**Huddersfield Town:** Alex Smithies, Andy Holdsworth, Michael Collins, Nathan Clarke, Danny Cadamarteri, Jim Goodwin, Phil Jevons (-82'), Robbie Williams, Andy Butler, Anthony Pilkington (-89'), Lionel Ainsworth (-60')
Subs: Ian Craney (+82'), Keigan Parker, Tom Clarke (+89'), Dominik Werling (+60'), Matt Glennon
**Peterborough United:** Joe Lewis, Russell Martin, Craig Morgan (-42'), Charlie Lee, Aaron McLean, George Boyd, Dean Keates (-46'), Craig Mackail-Smith, Paul Coutts, Chris Whelpdale (-85'),Gabriel Zakuani
Subs: Sergio Torres, Shaun Batt (+42'), Dominic Green (+85'), Andrew Crofts (+46'), Danny Blanchett

I love Huddersfield. I can see that it's not the most beautiful town in the world, but it's where I went to University, and for that reason alone it holds a special little place in my heart. Stepping out on to the platform at Huddersfield station brought back all those fond memories of University life. The best chips and cheese in the world, courtesy of our local take-away, Centro's. The cheapest chips and gravy in the world, courtesy of the Student Union; the dumb waiter that delivered the chips up a whole floor because the 'waitresses' were too old to carry a loaded plate up a flight of stairs at our local eat-in chippy (the name escapes me). I ate a lot of chips at University. Damn good chips. Leading up to the game though, I felt that the chips were down.

The previous weekend I'd watched us get spanked by Leeds whilst sat in front of someone who felt that shouting racist abuse towards Becchio was in no way hypocritical given our own Argentine was sat on the bench. This was followed by finding another section of our fans urinating in the sinks and under the hand dryers in the bogs whilst singing chants about the Leeds fans who were stabbed in Istanbul. It was enough to put my good friend Tim Knighton off football completely. I didn't feel quite the same, but I understood where he was coming from. That night I had contemplated giving up myself. I can live with Posh being crap and losing games, it's not like I'm not used to that. It was the behaviour of the fans that had upset me the most. That night I logged on to londonroad.net and found the thread where Darragh had responded to fans' questions. Despite my misgivings towards some of our fans, I felt that Darragh – the best chairman in the league by all accounts – was deserving of all the support we could give with him.

Given the way that Posh had previously responded to defeat, I was sure that the Huddersfield game was going to change everything. We were going to rip them to shreds. At the end of the game the fans would hail it the greatest victory of our 08/09 campaign, and sing the praises of the team that had played with passion, guile and skill that Huddersfield simply couldn't cope with. A couple of pints in a typically soulless Wetherspoon's with my regular match-day buddies only served to reassure me.

Sadly, Michael Collins' neat finish following an incisive passing move that cut straight through the middle of our defence after 35 mins, put paid to my hopes. There were some good moments, including the obligatory CMS one-on-one which he obviously failed to convert. But this looked like a team suffering a hangover from the previous weekend's defeat. The other chances that we created seemed to fall to Shaun Batt, who is no more of a footballer than I am, and is the one player who makes me doubt Fergie's ability to spot a player. Both Boyd and Green found him with decent crosses to the far post, but his heading/shooting ability is somehow worse than his ball control and the opportunities were wasted.

Batt was only on the pitch for more than his usual 20 minute cameo thanks to an injury to Craig Morgan. With the out-of-favour Blanchett also on the bench, the natural solution seemed to be to bring him on and move Charlie Lee into the centre, but instead Whelps was moved to right-back and Martin moved in to the centre. The goal was scored before this forced change, so you could argue that the make-shift defence performed well, but Huddersfield too had chances that they squandered, so I don't think the scoreline tells the full story, as is usually the case.

On the plus side, we sat right in front of three of the Posh WAGS for the majority of the game, and they proved a pleasant distraction from the disappointing display on the pitch. Did no one think to tell them that Huddersfield in January is bloody freezing though?

*Dave Nicholson*

* * * * *

**31/01/09**

| | | P | W | D | L | Pts |
|---|---|---|---|---|---|---|
| 1 | Leicester | 28 | 19 | 7 | 2 | 64 |
| 2 | MK Dons | 28 | 17 | 3 | 8 | 54 |
| | | | | | | |
| 4 | Posh | 28 | 14 | 8 | 6 | 50 |

# February

**02/02/09**

Manchester United centre back James Chester signs on a one-month loan deal. He is signed as cover for Craig Morgan who has been ruled out for two weeks with a toe injury.

* * * * *

**03/02/09**

The match at Brighton is postponed after heavy snow fall and freezing conditions. And a hurricane.

* * * * *

**05/02/09**

The home match against Carlisle United is postponed because of the continuing freezing conditions.

* * * * *

**06/02/09**

Lee Frecklington joins on a three-month loan deal from Lincoln City with a view to a permanent move in the summer.

* * * * *

**10/02/09**

## Brighton & Hove Albion 2-4 Peterborough Utd

| Brighton & Hove Albion | Peterborough Utd |
|---|---|
| Davies '27 | Mackail-Smith '38 |
| McNulty '45 | McLean '42 |
| | Keates '65 (pen.) |
| | McLean '76 |

Att:5,087.

**Brighton and Hove Albion:** John Sullivan, Adam Hinshelwood, Adam El-Abd, Jason Jarrett (-89'), Nicky Forster, Jimmy McNulty, Adam Virgo, Tommy Elphick (-86'), Craig Davies, Calvin Andrew, Sébastien Carole (-77')
Subs: Michel Kuipers, Dean Cox (+77'), Kevin McLeod (+89'), Dave Livermore, Tommy Fraser (+86')
**Peterborough United:** Joe Lewis, Russell Martin, Charlie Lee, Aaron McLean, George Boyd, Dean Keates,, Craig Mackail-Smith (-88'), Paul Coutts, Shaun Batt (-72'), Gabriel Zakuani, James Chester
Subs: Lee Frecklington (+88'), Chris Whelpdale (+72'), Dominic Green, Ben Wright, Danny Blanchett

At the time of this fixture I was 'lucky' enough to be working 10 miles down the road so a Tuesday night away game turned out to be the closest match I have ever travelled to in 37 years of following Posh.

Leaving work at five on the dot, I drove back to my hotel, changed in three minutes flat and ran to my car like a kid promised a trip to Toys R Us with a £100 voucher. I'd been pre-warned of the parking nightmare at Withdean Stadium (Stadium in the loosest possible sense) so I made straight for the ground to suss things out. Arriving at 6.20pm I saw the supporter's coach just pulling off and an assortment of Posh characters walking towards The Sportsman bar which is part of the complex. I slowed down and asked a steward the best place to park expecting the usual "follow the signs you muppet" response only to be met with an extremely friendly "hang on mate, we'll move these bollards and you can park where the bus was". What a result, thirty yards from the away end and twenty yards from the pub. I had a good feeling about tonight's game now.

A couple of pints later - even Des Lynam popped in to see who I was - and I decided I would take in the delights of the ground and grab a vegetarian pie because, as everyone knows, football grounds cater so well for the non-meat eating fraternity. I handed over my ticket and walked around the corner towards the away seating allocation.

Well, what can I say? How can I put it into words? Never, and I mean never, have I seen a football ground like it. An athletics track with scaffolding around it is the only way I can begin to describe it. If it hadn't been such a cold night I'm convinced a thousand flies would have flown into my mouth as I stood there aghast at what lay before me. I genuinely felt so sorry for Brighton supporters at that stage of the evening - but that soon passed.

I made my way to the burger van: "what you got without meat love?" I asked. "Chips or onions in a bun" was the response. Spoilt for choice I opted for the chips and was amazed that I got exactly 20 chips for £2. At 10p a chip I was determined to savour every last one. I sat on a concrete step and polished them off in about 90 secs.

As the teams made their way out from a portakabin right next to our end I made my way to the seats. I found an empty one at the back and couldn't believe how far away the pitch actually was. An eight lane running track, a dismantled high jump and a covered-up long jump sandpit were all clearly in view but as the players continued on their walk to the centre circle I found them getting smaller and smaller. Mumbling started amongst the Posh faithful such as "when are the players coming out" and "come on Posh if you're out there". £20 not to see is quite a lot of money when you think about it.

The game got underway with Posh kicking away from us. The goal at the far end may as well have been in Eastbourne for what I could see but fortunately, of the six goals to go in that night, four would be at our end.

Posh started shakily at the back and after 20mins or so a tame shot from the edge of the area spilled out of Lewis's grasp and their forward had an easy tap in to put Brighton one up. Oh dear, is this going to be a long night after all? Not likely, Coutts picked the ball up just inside their half and kicked it in a forward direction. A minute later Brighton were kicking off so the Posh fans went mental as it could only mean one thing, we've scored. Everybody went silent to hear the man on the tannoy tell us who had scored: "And the Peterborough equaliser is from Craig Mackail-Smith". "Yesssssss" went the Posh fans in unison and we all stamped our feet like lunatics and the whole scaffolding began to rattle.

Minutes later and Aaron McLean was running towards the corner flag with two or three Posh players chasing him. "Have we scored again?" asked a Posh fan. "Not sure, wait to see if Brighton kick off" came the response. Brighton did duly kick off and we again could take our enjoyment out on the scaffolding. Two-one and cruising at this stage and surely it was just a matter of how many? Then, on the stroke of half time Brighton win a corner, swing it over and their guy is left completely unmarked to knock it home. Two – two and the whistle goes so time for a visit to the gents.

On the way back to my seat a couple of Posh fans had gathered outside the portakabin at our end where all sorts of expletives were escaping the open windows. I wandered over, peered through and saw Darren Ferguson giving the seated Posh players the full Alex Ferguson hair dryer treatment. What he said and to whom will remain anonymous but fair to say it was real eye and ear opening stuff and I can't believe that the stewards left three or four of us there to witness the whole thing. However, his team talk almost had me reaching for my kit so the players themselves must have been itching to get back out and put things right, which they duly did.

With Posh attacking our end we could start to get into the game more and the volume from the away end began to build. George Boyd was ripping pieces out of their right back and on one run he actually sat three players on their arses. During another mazy run, Boyd drifted into the area and invited a tackle from a bewildered defender who was left with no choice but to trip him up. Double whammy here, a penalty to Posh and we could see it. Dean Keates stepped up and slammed the ball into the back of the net sending 200 odd Poshies into delirium. Ten minutes from time and McLean added another and it was all over.

A fine and much needed victory to push us closer to the promised land of the Championship. At the time of writing I'm not sure whether we will do it or not but one thing is for sure, if I ever have to go back to this ground then I'll sit with the Brighton fans just so I can see both ends of the pitch.

*Gary Miller*

* * * * *

**14/2/09**

## Peterborough Utd 1 - 3 Yeovil Town

McLean '56 — Warne '31, Brown '33, MacDonald '69

Att: 6,129 (340 away).

**Peterborough United:** Joe Lewis, Russell Martin, Charlie Lee (-19'), Aaron McLean, George Boyd, Dean Keates, Craig Mackail-Smith, Paul Coutts, Shaun Batt (-71'), Gabriel Zakuani, Danny Blanchett
Subs: Chris Whelpdale (+19'), Sergio Torres, Dominic Green (+71'), Ben Wright, Danny Andrew
**Yeovil Town:** Josh Wagenaar, Terry Skiverton (-41'), Jon Worthington, Andy Welsh (-72'), Craig Alcock, Paul Warne, Aaron Brown, Aleksandar Prijovi? (-59'), Shaun MacDonald, Lee Peltier, Nathan Smith
Subs: Nathan Jones (+72'), Gavin Tomlin (+59'), Luke Rodgers, Kieran Murtagh (+41'), Jordan Street

Awful, awful, awful. Two first-half goals conceded from almost identical set-pieces and then a shocker from Lewis to let in Yeovil's third just when Posh looked to be getting back into the game. Blame will be directed at the keeper but the team as a whole turned in an indifferent performance against willing but limited opposition.

*Larry Fly*

* * * * *

**17/02/09**

## Tranmere Rovers 1 - 1 Peterborough United

Barnett '16 Mackail-Smith '37

Att: 4,862.

**Tranmere Rovers:** John Achterberg, Ben Chorley, Antony Kay, Bas Savage, Ian Moore, Stephen Jennings, Gareth Edds, Edrissa Sonko (-63'), Aaron Cresswell, Charlie Barnett, Ryan Shotton
Subs: Terry Gornell, Luke Waterfall, Paul Henry, Chris Shuker (+63'), Peter Kennedy
**Peterborough United:** Joe Lewis, Russell Martin, Charlie Lee, Aaron McLean, George Boyd, Dean Keates, Craig Mackail-Smith, Paul Coutts, Chris Whelpdale (-34'), Gabriel Zakuani, James Chester
Subs: Lee Frecklington (+34'), Sergio Torres, Dominic Green, Ben Wright,Danny Blanchett

The clubs met for the 17th time this season. The formation we changed to when Frecklington replaced Whelpdale was 4-3-3 with CMS on the right and obviously Boyd on the left. Lewis did well and thankfully there were no dickheads heckling him. We should've wrapped the game up early in the second half as we were cutting them to ribbons time and again but there were a couple of bad finishes and on other occasions quite simply the wrong option was taken. We seemed to tire a lot towards the end and were fairly lucky to hold on. Overall though I'd say the draw was a fair result.

*Matt Squires*

*In these days of super-fit, awesomely-athletic footballers, it feels strange to report that the central character at Prenton Park last night turned out to be a portly, grey-haired geezer. Referee Phil Gibbs, who, in contrast to the usual despots with a whistle, officiated in the manner of a friendly uncle, gave Posh two huge reprieves during injury-time at the end of a pulsating encounter.*

*Alan Swann*
*The Evening Telegraph*

* * * * *

**21/02/09**

## Hereford United 0 - 1 Peterborough United

McLean '3

Att: 3,217 (364 away).

**Hereford United:** Gulácsi Péter, Richard Rose, Toumani Diagouraga, Kris Taylor, Febian Brandy, Steve Guinan, Sam Gwynne (-38'), Richard Jackson, Godwin Antwi, Sam Hewson, Jennison Myrie-Williams (-46')
Subs: Ben Smith (+46'), Matt Done, Simon Johnson (+38'), Michael D'Agostino, José Veiga
**Peterborough United:** Joe Lewis, Russell Martin, Charlie Lee (-55'), Lee Frecklington (-81'), Aaron McLean, George Boyd, Dean Keates, Craig Mackail-Smith, Paul Coutts, Gabriel Zakuani, James Chester
Subs: Chris Whelpdale (+81'), Sergio Torres, Dominic Green, Ben Wright, Danny Blanchett (+55')

In many ways this game has a certain symmetry. Like most of the Posh fans attending the fixture, we made the same journey last April to witness a 1-0 Posh victory that gained us promotion from League 2. Happy days! Once again I'm travelling with my mate Mark who is a Codicote Bull, a small, select group of long distance HUFC fans who take their name from the Hertfordshire village where they now live.

I have breakfast with my two boys and watch the previous nights Big League Weekend. There's a feature on Posh and an interview with Aaron McLean, who says his non-league background is a motivation to achieve success in League football. I really like this attitude. And there's more encouragement as he confirms the team's view that if they only 'do well' in League 1 then they will have achieved nothing, only promotion is going to register as success. The guest panel includes Bryan Gunn (Norwich City manager) who says from his experience Darragh MacAnthony would not consider selling his prize assets without a heavy premium price tag. This stuff just fills you full of pride, hope and ambition and gets you really up for the game.

Leaving St Albans I head north up the A1 to pick up Mark from Codicote, then it's off to Hereford. We chat about the usual stuff; work, football and the prospects for the game ahead. We both conclude it's likely to be close. We both predict 1-0 but predictably in opposite directions. Hereford have beaten Leeds 2-0 mid-week while Posh have won just 3 of their last 8 league games. A big game this.

We compare symmetrical injury lists. Hereford have several defenders out injured (after beating Cheltenham in a kicking competition) but have strengthened their squad with several loan players, including Febian Brandy from Man Utd. Meanwhile the Posh injury list features mostly defenders but we have strengthened the squad with Lee Frecklington, Ben Wright and James Chester.

We break the 130 mile journey with a pit stop at Susie's road side van on the A436 - in the lay-by opposite the Seven Springs restaurant - for the best bacon rolls going. Ballast is always good on long range trips. The last leg of the trip drags as the road narrows and winds but we arrive in Hereford around half twelve. It is the most glorious day and we declare it the first day of spring. For the first time in ages it's a pleasant temperature, which was underlined by the minimalist clothing being worn by the local females in Hereford town centre. Not that we looked.

In the Grapes we're joined by Andy (aka Iorfa) whom I met on the londonroad.net and after introductions, some banter and a pint we all head off to Edgar Street. We go direct to Legends, the Hereford club bar, which has over flowed into the car park to make the most of the sunshine. Andy and I are in Posh colours, which attracts friendly interest from the locals. A mystery Bulls fan shows us his chest tattoo and tells that he was prevented from going into Hereford for their mid-week victory over Leeds. I enquire if he was stopped by his wife or Police, his silence suggested the latter.

Mark heads to the home stands while Andy and I proceed to the curved away terrace and take a central position. As the teams run out you can't fail to spot that the strips are complete mirror images Hereford - white shirt, black shorts, white socks Posh - black shirt, white shorts, black socks. Ian Drury's Sweet Gene Vincent instantly springs to mind, but I take the choice of kits as another positive symmetrical omen.

Lee Frecklington has made the starting line up and plays very well. After just three minutes we are sent into raptures as McLean collects a beautifully weighted long ball from George Boyd and then has time to slot his shot past the keeper. Aaron did little to win the home fans over by celebrating his goal with a Bull impersonation, a fitting choice. Hereford fans haven't liked him since the 2004

Conference Play-Offs - an incident between Aaron (then playing for Aldershot) and Andy Tretton resulted in the Hereford player being dismissed. Long memories have Bulls. I text Mark in the home stand to share the moment, his reply is short. Further chances for Lee, McLean and Martin follow before half-time

Straight after the break the game should have been made secure, but Mackail-Smith steered the ball wide from three yards out when scoring seemed the easier option. Hereford grew in confidence and possession during the second-half but they were unable to convert their opportunities, although the game had a dramatic ending with Joe Lewis fouling Febian Brandy in a dangerous position. James Chester dealt with the incoming free kick and Posh took a crucial three points home.

1-0 to Posh away at Hereford. I like symmetry me.

*Chris Sharpe*

* * * * *

**24/02/09**

## Peterborough United 1 - 0 Carlisle United

McLean '69

Att: 5,103 (267 away).

**Peterborough United:** Joe Lewis, Russell Martin, Charlie Lee, Lee Frecklington (-44'), Aaron McLean, George Boyd, Dean Keates, Craig Mackail-Smith, Paul Coutts, Gabriel Zakuani (-17', James Chester
Subs: Shane Blackett (+17'), Chris Whelpdale (+44'), Sergio Torres, Dominic Green, Ben Wright

**Carlisle United:** Ben Williams, Peter Murphy, Danny Graham, Paul Thirlwell, Joe Anyinsah (-72'), Cleveland Taylor, Lewis Neal (-82'), Richard Keogh, Graham Kavanagh, Tony Kane, Michael Liddle

Subs: David Raven, Chris Lumsdon, Michael Bridges (+82′), Scott Dobie (+72′), Gary Madine

Originally scheduled for the 7 February this fixture became a casualty of the snow and a frozen pitch, so hence a revised mid-week date. I've arranged to work from home so that I can make a prompt departure to ensure making kick off. Although it's only a 67 mile trip from St Albans, the A1(M) northbound around Stevenage is always a challenge midweek.

I'm travelling with my elder sister Melanie and her fella Mark (a Carlisle fan) who are driving to the game from London. They pick me up bang on 5pm. Eager, very eager. We quickly get into discussing the prospects for the match, and despite Carlisle losing to Stockport at the weekend Mark is upbeat and calls 2-0 for the visitors; I go for 2-1 to Posh whilst Melanie predicts a 3-0 cruise for Posh. Bets placed we inch past Stevenage.

We arrive, park then stroll to Charters for a beer. Oakham Ales JHB hits the spot and as I'm not driving for once I have a couple more. The barge is it's usual busy self on match days and Mark spots some Carlilse away strips amongst the crowd. The atmosphere is building and we join the stream of people making their way across the Bridge to London Road.

We take up position in the upper section of the Glebe Road/Family/South stand and meet regulars Nick and Richard. Mark is keeping his allegance low profile and my sister is enjoying his discomfort.

Posh make a lively start and a slick move involving Charlie Lee, George Boyd and Craig Mackail-Smith was only thwarted by defender Peter Murphy. Gabriel Zakuani heads a Paul Coutts corner just wide of the post. On nine minutes an aerial challenge in the Posh box had the whole ground gasping as Zakuani landed head first. It looked horrific. The game was halted for 7 minutes whilst a neck brace was fitted and carefully Zak was stretchered off the field to go directly to hospital.

So with Zak out of the game Shane Blackett came on - his first appearance since dislocating his shoulder (again) when playing against errrr..... Carlisle in October. Carlisle try to capitalise and come close with a Lewis Neal free kick floating over our back four which Danny Graham volleys goalwards but Joe Lewis is up to the task and blocks it with a heel. We repeatedly counter and Paul Coutts and Lee have long range attempts, whilst Mackail-Smith has a penalty claim turned down. Things go from bad to worse two minutes into first-half stoppage time when Lee Frecklington limps off with a hamstring injury and is replaced by Chris Whelpdale.

The second half starts as lively as the first ended, with both sides enjoying chances at each end. Charlie Lee stands out as he both drives us forward and shores up the defence. The game is decided when Lee picks out Whelpdale whose fierce shot rebounds off the Carlisle keeper and Aaron McLean slots it home to earn, on balance, a deserved victory.

That's 5 goals in 5 matches for Aaron, and Posh are now just one point behind MK Dons. Later a text update informs us that Zak has not sustained a fracture - which is the best news of all.

*Chris Sharpe*

**28/02/09**

## Peterborough United 1 - 2 Southend United

Keates '6 (pen.) — Christophe '25, Blackett '63 (o.g.)

Att: 7,341 (887 away).

**Peterborough United:** Joe Lewis, Russell Martin, Shane Blackett, Charlie Lee, Aaron McLean, George Boyd, Dean Keates, Craig Mackail-Smith, Chris Whelpdale (-64'), Tommy Williams (-86'), James Chester
Subs: James McKeown, Sergio Torres (+64'), Dominic Green, Ben Wright (+86'), Danny Blanchett
**Southend United:** Steve Mildenhall, Dorian Dervite, Peter Clarke, Adam Barrett, Anthony Grant, Alan McCormack, Lee Barnard (-88'), Franck Moussa, Osei Sankofa, Theo Robinson (-89'), Jean-François Christophe
Subs: Simon Francis (+88'), Johnny Herd, Kevin Betsy (+89'), Ian Joyce, Stuart O'Keefe

A performance that sums up a month of fluctuating quality from the Posh. A brilliant start and an early lead is then squandered as chances are missed and passes start to go astray. Without Zakuani and Morgan Posh look less than solid at the back and the hapless - I'm sure he's been called that elsewhere in this book - Blackett slices into his own net under no apparent pressure. But whatever the defensive frailties Posh still had chances to win this game and that is probably the most disappointing aspect of the result.

*Mike Hunt*

* * * * *

**29/02/09**

| | | P | W | D | L | Pts |
|---|---|---|---|---|---|---|
| 1 | Leicester | 34 | 21 | 11 | 2 | 74 |
| 2 | MK Dons | 32 | 19 | 5 | 8 | 62 |
| 3 | Posh | 34 | 17 | 9 | 8 | 60 |

# *March*

**03/03/09**

## Leyton Orient 2 - 3 Peterborough United

| Leyton Orient | Peterborough United |
|---|---|
| McGleish '42 | Whelpdale '6 |
| McGleish '56 | Torres '12 |
| | Martin '45 |

Att: 3,381 (688 away).

**Leyton Orient:** Jamie Jones, Stephen Purches, Tamika Mkandawire, Adam Chambers, Sean Thornton, Andrew Cave-Brown, Jason Demetriou, Jimmy Smith (-46'), Jordan Spence, Scott McGleish, Simon Church (-72')
Subs: Glenn Morris, Brian Saah, Wayne Gray (+72'), Dean Morgan (+46'), Paul Terry

**Peterborough United:** Joe Lewis, Russell Martin, Chris Westwood, Charlie Lee, Aaron McLean, George Boyd (-89'), Dean Keates, Paul Coutts, Chris Whelpdale (-76'), Tommy Williams, Sergio Torres
Subs: Shane Blackett, Craig Mackail-Smith (+76'), James McKeown, Shaun Batt (+89'), Dominic Green

Having lost, and played badly, against Southend at the weekend it was with some trepidation that I arrived at Peterborough station for the short journey down to London. Our plan was for two of us to catch a fast train while the other four would be taking the 11.44 slow train, collecting four more lads in St. Neots. Fortunately the 11.44 was cancelled so all six of us were able to catch the fast train, waving at St. Neots as we passed, and reminisce about *Zulu* and away days gone by.

We arrived in Kings Cross and 20 mins later were supping our first pint at The Sir John Oldcastle in Farringdon. Soon the St. Neots lads arrived closely followed by Hillingdon Posh, making us a group of eleven. Three hours, six beers, a bit of food and lots of chat later it was time to make our way to Leyton.

Leaving Leyton tube station Boozy decided to make a closer inspection of the stairs and was helped back to his feet by a kind West Indian gentleman much to the amusement of the rest of us who were following behind. Boozy's job was to lead us to the Birkbeck Tavern, aparently a real old-fashioned London pub. Unfortunately in the rain and fading light we couldn't find it and ended up in another establishment, no idea what it was called and the landlord couldn't find it on a map either! From there we made our way to the Coach & Horses on Leyton High Road for a final beer or two before the game. By now the wind was howling and rain was coming down in sheets, making us think it would be a tough evening to play football.

As for the game, it was an absolute cracker. Craig Mackail-Smith was surprisingly relegated to the subs bench and Chris Westwood was in at centre back. Within 15 mins Posh were two up following a Chris Whelpdale header and a Sergio Torres shot that the Orient keeper somehow managed to let squeeze under his body. The rain was now forgotten and I fully expected Posh to win by a country mile. Unfortunately Orient had other ideas as they pulled a goal back on 42 mins through Scott McGleish following the harsh award of a penalty. Posh didn't let their heads drop and within 3 mins restored their two-goal advantage thanks to a Russell Martin header from a Paul Coutts corner.

The second half started brightly with Posh missing a good opportunity but then, on 56 mins McGleish, always a quality player, coolly slotted home from a cross after the referee had overruled the linesman and awarded Orient a free-kick, even though he was 50 yards away from the incident. Now we were in for a very nervy 25 mins as Orient launched ball after ball into the wind and rain to try and get an equalizer. Charlie Lee and Westwood were solid at the back, covering for each other and snuffing out everything Orient could throw at them. Then, in injury time, Orient were awarded a free-kick just outside the penalty area. The free-kick was pretty poor but given the conditions Joe Lewis was only able to knock the shot straight to an opposition player no more than six yards from goal. As we feared the worst Joe Lewis stood tall and blocked the goal-bound shot following which the referee thankfully blew for full-time.

To celebrate we stopped off for a quick pint at Liverpool Street Station then made our way to Kings Cross. Walking to the station Boozy realized he had left his wallet at Liverpool Street so he and Adi returned to collect it while I caught the fast train to Peterborough.

Thanks to a points failure at Stevenage, or some similar excuse, the journey took far too long but at least the rain had stopped for my walk back to Stanground. I was in bed for 2.00am and spent most of the following day with little voice and a rather sore head, these are the matches that remind me why I fly 4,000 miles to support the Posh.

*Steve Bull*

* * * * *

**07/03/09**

## Hartlepool United 1 - 2 Peterborough United

Monkhouse '38 — Keates '11, Boyd '48

Att: 3,722 (337 away).

**Hartlepool United:** Arran Lee-Barratt, Ritchie Humphreys, Michael Nelson, Sam Collins, Gary Liddle, Andy Monkhouse, Ben Clark, Antony Sweeney, David Foley, Michael Mackay (-70'), Keigan Parker
Subs: Joel Porter (+70'), Alan Power, Jonny Rowell, Mark Cook, Liam Henderson
**Peterborough United:** Joe Lewis, Russell Martin, Chris Westwood, Charlie Lee, Aaron McLean, George Boyd, Dean Keates, Paul Coutts, Chris Whelpdale, Sergio Torres (-66'), Gabriel Zakuani
Subs: Shane Blackett, Craig Mackail-Smith (+66'), James McKeown, Tommy Williams, Dominic Green

Not a place to drive to is Hartlepool. I once returned to our mini-bus to discover it had been relieved of its windscreen.

So this season I decided with my apprentice, young Ant, to travel up there by train. At the station we had the dubious pleasure of meeting up with some lads from Bourne who suggested we stop at York for a 'few' on the way, as anyone who has visited Hartlepool and York will testify there really is no comparison between the two places - well there is but Hartlepool suffers badly.

We jumped off at York after checking the train times for our onward journey and aimed to get the 12.15 to Hartlepool, if we missed that there were further trains at 13.00, 13.25 and 13.45 and the last one only got us in at 14.50 so common sense dictated we caught a train no later than 13.00 just to be safe. I imagine you've already guessed which one we actually caught. After hitting Budgens for a few tinnies we made our way to the station for, yep the 13.45.

We arrived at Hartlepool only five minutes before kick off and walking seemed too much effort and so we piled into a couple of taxis and off we went. The £2.40 minimum charge on the meter went up to £2.70 as the taxi pulled up outside the ground. Well, it doesn't cost much for a 700 yard journey does it!

After chatting to a bloke called Geordie who I'd not seen for about 10 years ( he is actually from Hartlepool but has supported Posh for most of his life after seeing us beat Newcastle at St James' Park in '62) we made our way into the ground and were slightly disappointed to see only about 400 fellow Posh fans. However, a good atmosphere was being generated and things improved even more when I went for something to eat, asked for a hot dog and the young girl produced a foot long hot dog with chips.

Not being a big eater I struggled through and settled down to watch the mighty Posh swarm over the struggling Pool but as so often with football in general and Posh in particular it didn't quite work out that way. We went ahead through a superb free kick from Keates. It hit the back of the net just as I told my apprentice that there was no way he'd score from there. A cock-up between Coutts,

Whelps and Lewis gifted them an equaliser but needless to say Joe got the blame both at the match and on the website all the next week.

That well known Scotsman, George McBoyd, scored a winner early on in the second half but we owed the win in the main to young Zak for some inspired defending especially right at the end when he risked the wellbeing of his head, neck and face to clear a shot off the line. He was probably highly peeved to learn as he got to his feet that the forward had already been flagged offside.

Having almost recovered from our pre-match refreshments we managed the five minute walk into town and knowing that there was over an hour until the train was due we pondered the wisdom of visiting the local hostelries as the natives are not known for their friendliness after a defeat.

Pop however stuck his head in a small but beautifully formed social club that was almost empty and they agreed to take our money for a while. The locals were friendly and a few ales were sunk whilst chatting about the relative merits of Posh and Pool. We then got onto the subject of when Middlesbrough used the Victoria Ground for a while when they were struggling - ooh the monkey hangers don't like them.

After purchasing some tinnies for the trip back to York we took our place on the train which contained a fair sprinkling of Spurs and Sunnerlan' supporters travelling back from the hilariously named Stadium of Light. We had a giggle with them but the main fun was had when two females were sent to our carriage apparently to check out there'd be no trouble though quite what they'd have done I do not know.

I asked them if they would pronounce five special words so that everyone could hear what a difference there was between a North-East pronunciation and the way normal folk speak. Constantinople comes out as Constantinuuurple. Kawasaki, incontrovertible and taramasalata followed. And then my personal favourite: the type of photographic film we all used on holiday which they pronounced as kurdak curlur gooooolllldddd. Fantastic.

After that enjoyable part of the journey we jumped off at York station for an hour and found some great company with two very drunk couples who had in theory been shopping but had obviously had a drink after every purchase, we serenaded them a few times with various Posh songs before making our farewells and catching the train home.

We purchased some more cans for the trip and as we had pre-booked made our way to coach D. Unfortunately it had been designated the 'quiet carriage'. Big mistake! As we got in and saw the looks of horror on those already enjoying the peaceful journey thus far we all shhhhhd each other which was not a good start as that was quite loud, then disaster hit.

Pop discovered that his tray on the back of the seat in front needed some WD 40 as it made an awful squeaking noise each time it was moved, needless to say this appealed to the devil inside and he proceeded to move the tray at regular intervals. This went on for some time and eventually one of the couples we had met at the station came in the carriage to warn us that the guard was preparing to call the police and that we'd be met by them at Doncaster. Now I've had some good nights in Donny it must be said but after such a long day I'd rather have been at home so we made our way to a carriage better suited to us.

Upon entering this new carriage we spotted some football shirts but could not work out who the hell they were, Turned out to be Brechin bloody City but even funnier than that was the fact that those five lads and a girl (kind of, she made Ann Widdecombe look like a model) were from Sixfingeredshire. Needless to say we took the piss, although in her case nature had got there an awfully long time before us.

Across the aisle from these unfortunates was a party of five very attractive young ladies, certainly compared to Mrs Mong anyway. I introduced ourselves to them explaining we'd been to football and it turned out they were American students returning from a day out in Edinburgh and York. I explained to them that whilst Edinburgh Castle was quite attractive it was nothing compared to Crowland Abbey and that Peterborough Cathedral was infinitely more beautiful than York Minster.

Someone asked them where their home university was and when they replied Salt Lake City I, being an educated man knew they were Mormons and so as a life-long atheist my fun began. "You do realise there is no God don't you?" was my opening gambit which I think is fair to say was not what they were expecting.

Once we'd got over that hurdle I asked how could it be right that five attractive young ladies such as themselves could not enjoy sex or alcohol? They explained how God fulfilled them so much that they had no need of those two experiences. Looking at the state of her from wobbs land across the aisle I could understand the sex opinion and then looking around the carriage at the representatives from Posh I accepted the anti-alcohol argument 100%. Indeed I was on the verge of booking a flight to Salt Lake City until Pop passed me another can of Stella.

The girls very gently let me down when I invited them to a Posh match and didn't seem too annoyed when I offered to fulfil them in a lot nicer way then God ever could. To be fair I am pretty sure my standard of luuurrrrvemaking, which is patchy at best, may well have been somewhat affected by the amount of beer I had consumed. Their very pleasant company which lets face it was a cut above that which I had shared all day (no offence lads) made the last part of a very long day go a lot quicker than would have been expected, certainly if the police been called onto the train at Donny.

This season has been one of the best I have ever known as a Posh fan and if only one of those five Vestal Virgins had agreed to accept my kind offer it would have gone down - phnarr phnarr - as truly the best, but then again they are Mormons not Morons.

A great day, an expensive day, but most importantly a day that hours before I got home and collapsed into bed, saw the mighty Posh get another three points.

*Adi Mowles.*

* * * * *

**10/03/09**

## Peterborough United 2 - 1 Scunthorpe United

Whelpdale '63 Lansbury '39
Mackail-Smith '86

Att: 5,637 (396 away).

**Peterborough United:** Joe Lewis, Russell Martin, Chris Westwood (-46'), Charlie Lee, Aaron McLean, George Boyd, Dean Keates, Paul Coutts, Chris Whelpdale, Sergio Torres (-46'), Gabriel Zakuani
Subs: Craig Mackail-Smith (+46'), James McKeown, Tommy Williams (+46'), Dominic Green, Ben Wright
**Scunthorpe United:** Joe Murphy, Joseph Mills (-58'), Cliff Byrne, Paul Hayes, Gary Hooper (-51'), David Mirfin, Grant McCann, Sam Togwell, Kevan Hurst, Krystian Pearce, Henri Lansbury (-72')
Subs: Matt Sparrow (+72'), Josh Lillis, Andrew Wright (+58'), Liam Trotter, Kayode Odejayi (+51')

There is something special, or at least different, about mid-week early Spring games. The crowd seems bigger than it actually is, the noise generated louder than usual, the pitch a sparkling crisper green and the ball seems to zip along the turf with more pace and precision. The players seem to pick up on this mood and raise their game.

Except they didn't, well at least not Posh in the first half. We were played off the park. Chris Westwood - such a calming and dominant influence when deputising for the injured Morgan over the previous month - was given the run-around by the excellent Hayes and Hooper. Posh seemed unable to keep the ball for any length of time and Scunthorpe should have been out of sight by half-time such was their dominance.

The manager acted decisively. Westwood was replaced by Williams, with Lee moving into the centre and Mackail-Smith - on the bench for the third game in a row - replaced Torres. Williams made a difference as he kept overlapping and freeing space up for Boyd. Lee began to drive forward and the previously anonymous Keates and Coutts took control of midfield. Williams began to whip in cross after cross - with that exaggerated Pieterson-esque follow through of his left foot - and The Iron began to buckle. Eventually Whelpdale, drifting in at the far post pulled Posh level and the noise went up a notch or four.

Posh poured forward as Scunthorpe were pinned back in their own half. Even the surly teenager a few seats away from me, who'd spent the first half playing on his mobile, was now up on his feet and roaring encouragement as the atmosphere grew increasingly fevered. With only a few minutes remaining Williams curved another cross into the box, Lee got to it first and though Murphy parried, Mackail-Smith was on hand to lash it into the net. Pandemonium.

I'm really starting to believe now.

*Paul Mitchell*

The first half was depressing. It was like watching a re-run of us being given a football lesson by West Brom. Scunthorpe could trap the ball and pass it to their own players - we were capable of doing neither. The only surprise was that their goal took as long to come as it did. The only bright moments were one or two nice touches from Whelpdale and some cool headed play from Coutts.

Most of the clearances out of defence were panic stricken and the negative passing became infuriating.

I think a few eyebrows were raised when Tom Williams was brought on, but I think he was one of the main reasons why the game changed out of all recognition. The other reason was that it suddenly became obvious that Ferguson banned Keates from taking any more corners in favour of Coutts; in fact Coutts had to run across the field at one point to take successive corners from different sides of the pitch.

Coutts was having an excellent game and when he started to break forward, Boyd was also getting more opportunities. He wasn't as influential as he can be, but with Coutts, Whelpdale and Williams all providing some decent balls, we suddenly became much more of a threat. Some of our clearances were still awful, but we were getting lucky bounces of the ball far more than in the first half and at times, Scunthorpe must have wondered what had hit them.

Even so, we still looked worryingly vulnerable to long ball tactics, something that has become a bit of a recurring problem this season. I have to feel sorry for Torres in a way, but he just didn't make enough of an impact to make himself an automatic choice for the starting line-up. If only Williams could be as effective as that in every game.

So, Saturday. Cobblers. It's going to be massive.

*Hugh Janus*

*"I still believe we are in with a great chance of winning this league. The plan is coming together, we planned for this and it is testament to the management and the players that we have put*

*ourselves in with a chance. You have to have bottle at this stage of the season and I believe Peterborough United are showing plenty of bottle."*

*Darragh MacAnthony*

* * * * *

**14/03/09**

## Peterborough United 1 - 0 Northampton Town
Lee '33

Att: 8,881 (1,793 away).

**Peterborough United:** Joe Lewis, Russell Martin, Charlie Lee, Aaron McLean, George Boyd (-88'), Dean Keates, Craig Mackail-Smith (-89'), Paul Coutts, Chris Whelpdale, Tommy Williams, Gabriel Zakuani (-7')
Subs: Chris Westwood (+88'), James McKeown, Sergio Torres, Shaun Batt (+89'), Dominic Green
**Northampton Town:** Chris Dunn, Jason Crowe, Danny Jackman, Mark Hughes, Carl Magnay (-46'), Chris Doig (-74'), Giles Coke, Colin Larkin, Andy Holt (-63'), Ikechi Anya, Abdul Osman
Subs: Leon Constantine (+63'), Liam Davis (+46'), Luke Guttridge, Paul Rodgers (+74'), Paul Walker

Living in Rushden for the majority of my life I have had both the good fortune and misfortune to have friends with six fingers and webbed toes. They may be good at counting and fast at swimming but they have to put up with watching that sh*te in claret every week.

The banter this year was almost non-existent prior to the big derby day as they knew their team was poor and they were due a spanking. Only Gilbert, who always has an opinion, was in typical mood and started his moaning just over a week before the big game. After the postponed Wobbs vs MK Dons game I got a text from Gilbert: "bollox, you lucky bastards, Bayo now misses your game". Quite why he's pinning his hopes on a bloke who is frankly fatter and slower than me - and that's saying something - is beyond me but that's his excuse and he's sticking by it. The usual £10 bet was made even though I'm still waiting for him to pay up after all the other times we've beaten them.

Finally the day arrived and it was an early start as the PUSFC (the Posh fans team). We had a match against the Wobbs in the morning so there was a chance to put one over them early and to complete the double after our 2-1 victory away earlier in the season. Having found ourselves 3-0 down with less than a half to go we put in a magnificent second half performance and eventually ran out 4-3 winners. What a result and a nice start to the day. Off to Ebs for a pre-match beer and then on to London Road for the big game.

Posh stroked the ball around nicely in the first couple of mins and it looked like we could be in for a cricket score but then it all went wrong when Zakuani was sent off for what was deemed a professional foul on the Wobbler striker with the green slippers on. A minute or two later and Wobbs hit the woodwork – cue a text from Gilbert "lucky bastards" – just as I was reading the text McLean hit the post for Posh so I sent the message straight back to him.

That shot gave me and many others hope as even though the Wobbs looked useless, 10 men vs 11 was always going to be tough for 85 minutes. On the half hour mark Charlie Lee popped up with what was to be the winning goal with a good header from a Paul Coutts cross and the Posh faithful erupted.

The Wobbs put pressure on the Posh during the second half which was to be expected and they hit the post and had one effort cleared off the line but this Posh team are made of sterner stuff these days and with heart, effort and commitment held on to their lead and took the three points thank you very much. A few of my six fingered friends agreed that we deserved the three points and Gilbert came out with the usual nonsense: "we were robbed, the ref was sh*t, we've got more fingers than you, we beat you last year etc." My response: "we'll never play you again."

*Dave Fitzjohn*

*10 men, we only need 10 men.*

* * * * *

**21/03/09**

## Bristol Rovers 0 - 1 Peterborough United

McLean '70

Att: 7,103 (466 away).

**Bristol Rovers:** Steve Phillips, Joe Jacobson, Chris Lines (-66'), Steve Elliott, Rickie Lambert, Darryl Duffy (-66'), Jeff Hughes (-83'), David Pipe, Byron Anthony, Craig Disley, Aaron Lescott
Subs: Craig Hinton, Stuart Campbell (+66'), Jo Kuffour (+66'), Sean Rigg (+83'), Danzelle St Louis-Hamilton
**Peterborough United:** Joe Lewis, Russell Martin, Chris Westwood, Charlie Lee, Aaron McLean, George Boyd, Dean Keates, Craig Mackail-Smith, Paul Coutts, Chris Whelpdale, Tommy Williams (-89')
Subs: Shane Blackett (+89'), James McKeown, Sergio Torres, Shaun Batt, Danny Blanchett

After last week's stunning performance against Cobblers and a nostalgic moment with big Jim Hall the Posh head for the West Country without Zak and Morgs to face Bristol Rovers and sharpshooter Ricky Lambert. Will they make it six wins out of seven and cement a late push for automatic promotion?

The Tom Tom was set and the scenic route was chosen. As we passed over Junction 13 we saw the first omen of the day - not a double Eddie but a dead fox in the road - well, it had to mean something.

Heading on towards Buckingham we encountered the MK licker picking up fans on their way to Yeovil. They were obviously attracted by the pie, pint, and a woman for a quid package on offer as they bundled on to the coach.

Bathboroboy had organised the drinks and as I headed for the pub. I knew things were not good as he jumped into the car at the traffic lights and said they wont let us in but we can park there. Best one I've heard, free parking but you can't buy our beer. We walked back to the Wellington where we met loadsa Poshies who had been let out for the day. Banter followed with the slightly deluded Rovers fans confident after scoring five the week before but nobody was brave enough to predict a nine goal thriller like earlier in the season.

The game kicked off and the commitment of the Posh players was outstanding. CMS should have had a couple but his one-on-one history came back to haunt him. Chris Westwood and Charlie Lee were outstanding at the back making sure that Lambert didn't get a sniff.

The second half was as tense as the first. I could see a Rovers goal in every attack but Westwood and Lee stayed strong. McLean and CMS were working tirelessly up front and our prayers were answered when the ball broke to McLean who didn't need a second chance goalllllllllllllllllllllllllllll

We had a foot in the Championship. Rovers gave us a couple of heart-stopping moments in the last five mins but it was meant to be, this was a big win. The players came over with Darren to receive the applause they deserved it and as we left the ground I selected Westwood as MoM, Matty selected Lee, nobody would have been wrong as they all played out of their skins.

We headed to the pub as the scores came through MK lose, Leicester draw, shame Millwall come back to beat Hartlepool but we would have taken those results at the start of the day.

We passed the MK licker just after Oxford, they didn't look happy. I overtook the coach singing along to Timi Yuro: "It may be over for you but it'll never be over for me."

*Paul Richardson*

* * * * *

**26/03/09**

*"Peterborough were on a good run but we wiped the floor with them in December, and I hope we can do the same this time. They are a good side but we are top and, if we turn up with our A game, we should be okay."*

*Nicky Adams, Leicester City*

* * * * *

**28/03/09**

## Peterborough United 2 - 0 Leicester City

Lee '44
Whelpdale '79

Att: 14,110 (4,054 away)

**Peterborough United:** Joe Lewis, Russell Martin, Charlie Lee, Aaron McLean, George Boyd, Dean Keates, Craig Mackail-Smith (-89'), Paul Coutts, Chris Whelpdale, Tommy Williams, Gabriel Zakuani
Subs: Shane Blackett, Chris Westwood, James McKeown, Sergio Torres, Shaun Batt (+89')
**Leicester City:** Tony Warner, Patrick Kisnorbo, Kerrea Gilbert, Matthew Oakley, Lloyd Dyer (-71'), Matty Fryatt, Max Gradel, Joe Mattock, Jack Hobbs, Paul Dickov, Bruno Berner (-61')
Subs: Michael Morrison, Nicky Adams (+71'), Barry Hayles (+61'), Wayne Brown, David Stockdale

With high winds and hail battering supporters and players alike a capacity crowd saw Posh defeat Leicester comprehensively. A 2-0 victory inspired by energetic performances from Lee, CMS, Williams and Boyd.

My uncle Gerald is a Leicester City season ticket holder. I once went with him to see them play Chelsea at Filbert Street, when Gianfranco Zola was still playing, but I'd never seen Leicester play Posh. When the Foxes beat Posh 4-0 at Christmas he was straight on the phone as payback for my jubilation when they were relegated months before. Uncle Gerald's view of this game was already pessimistic the week before, so he did his best to sound unsurprised when Posh won the game employing his brand of sarcasm and clutching at the thinnest of straws with regard to this being our biggest game of the season.

Leicester's strategy for this game was ruined by an early booking for time wasting by Tony Warner. If only other referee's had been as prompt in dealing with this during some of our other matches this season. A Lee challenge seconds later resulted in a booking for him and the game began to take on the familiar dimension of the local derby. Paul Dickov, a player so annoying he could goad the Dalai Lama into a rage, was a notable presence on the pitch impeding Joe Lewis at a corner and generally cheating. Dickov was the replacement for Steve Howard, whose injury meant he was unable to provide the usual foil for dangerous striker Fryatt.

But it was Lee that shone and his goal just before half-time was sublime. A scrappy windy first half ended in a hail storm, through which burst Charlie Lee. Ignoring an opportunity to pass he threw a deft dummy before turning, beating one man, then two before curling a shot into the top left corner of the Leicester goal. The goal was met with a huge roar and the dream of becoming Champions gained new life.

Posh came out early as usual for the second half, as did Leicester, who probably thought they would appear first. Fergie's much proclaimed need for tempo was evident from the start with Posh the stronger of the two teams with a succession of corners, free kicks and chances being created for McLean and CMS. Dickov, ever the team player, proceeded to snipe at Arsenal loanee Gilbert for giving away a free kick on the edge of the Leicester area and the two had to be separated. As a Poshie, there is no better sight than the opposition losing it. Unfortunately Fergie lost it too, after a foul on Whelpdale, and an angry tirade aimed at the assistant referee led to him being sent to the stand for the rest of the match.

The London Road crowd noise increased in volume and another quality Posh move resulted in a Keates free kick hitting the bar. Minutes later with the wind still howling around the stadium, a Boyd clearance resulted in a beautiful piece of control by CMS who then beat two men and played the ball across the pitch to Chris Whelpdale who drilled the ball into the bottom corner. 2-0. At this point I turned to the man next at me and shook him. I don't know who he was and I apologise. Chants of We are going up and We're just too good for you rang around the stadium.

The Christmas defeat didn't matter, but this result did. Posh went through March taking maximum points. The bet I made in August was still very much alive and Charlie Lee confirmed his status as a terrace hero.

*Steve Turner*

As if scoring the winner against Northampton wasn't enough, Charlie Lee may just have written his name into Posh folklore once more. This time, it was a delightful goal, backed up by a sensational 90 minutes of defensive dominance, that caused London Road to sing his name in unison.

With the nation listening on FiveLive, Posh took all three points against the division's top side, Leicester City. Posh had been thoroughly panned in the away fixture, losing 4-0 to a team seemingly destined for the title. And in the early stages of the London Road encounter, a slightly makeshift Leicester looked bright, with veteran striker

Paul Dickov putting himself about with all the charm of a serial puppy-drowner.

But then the sky went dark, the wind whipped up and, as the hail lashed down at a 45° angle, sending the occupants of the family stand into a mad scramble for cover, it was Posh who better weathered the storm. The home side took the game to the table-topping visitors, forcing a corner which led to man of the match Lee's sensational opener. The battling cheeky chappy wrong-footed his hapless marker, drifted past two equally bemused Leicester defenders and fired the ball across Tony Warner and inside the far post.

Half-time followed, the sky brightened, then quickly resumed its torrent of ice pellets, and, as play resumed, it was Posh who looked the more dangerous side. McLean and Mackail-Smith terrorised the sodden City cloggers, who were reduced to fighting among themselves such was their frustration. Mackail-Smith showed all the running we've come to expect - as well as the disappointing finishing from one-on-ones we've become accustomed to.

But he's not one to let things like that get hm down, and it was a typically direct run from CMS, and incisive pass, that created the killer goal for Chris Whelpdale. Whelpdale collected the ball, took a touch and, from a tight angle, kept his composure to drill the ball low into the far corner. It was a well deserved goal from a man really starting to blossom into a fine footballer. Whelpdale looked assured, confident, mature - everything you could ask from your players in such a big match.

And so it ended. 2-0. With Joe Lewis barely troubled by the once free-scoring Fryatt and ageing nasty piece of work

Dickov. For that he can thank Zakuani and Lee, both imperious in the centre of defence, while Keates and Coutts continued to forge a successful partnership in the middle of the park - Keates directing play and putting a foot in front of any Leicester breakaway, Coutts a visionary ball-player with the ability to change the flow of the game in a single pass.

With Milton Keynes losing to Leeds, Millwall have emerged as the strongest threat to Posh's automatic promotion hopes. But, on the strength of this game, perhaps it will be the Foxes who are more readily checking over their shoulder for the chasing pack.

*LondonRoad.net*

* * * * *

**31/03/09**

## Millwall 0 - 1 Colchester

Platt 84

Clive Platt finally scores a goal for Posh. Good work big man.

* * * * *

**31/03/09**

| | | P | W | D | L | Pts |
|---|---|---|---|---|---|---|
| 1 | Leicester | 40 | 23 | 13 | 4 | 82 |
| 2 | Posh | 40 | 23 | 9 | 8 | 78 |
| 3 | Millwall | 39 | 22 | 9 | 10 | 69 |

# *April*

**04/04/09**

## Oldham Athletic 1 - 2 Peterborough United

| Oldham Athletic | Peterborough United |
| --- | --- |
| Taylor '43 | Mackail-Smith '26 |
| | Mackail-Smith '86 |

Att: 5,083 (977 away).

**Oldham Athletic:** Shane Supple, Neil Eardley, Danny Whitaker, Mark Allott, Reuben Hazell, Kevin Maher, Sean Gregan, Chris Taylor, Daniel Jones, Lewis Alessandra (-69'), Ian Westlake
Subs: Stefan Stam, Greg Fleming, Matthew Wolfenden (+69'), Kieran Lee, Paul Black
**Peterborough United:** Joe Lewis, Russell Martin, Charlie Lee, Aaron McLean, George Boyd, Dean Keates, Craig Mackail-Smith, Paul Coutts, Chris Whelpdale (-63'), Tommy Williams (-84'), Gabriel Zakuani (-82')
Subs: Shane Blackett (+84'), Chris Westwood (+82'), James McKeown, Sergio Torres, Shaun Batt (+63')

After the run of tight wins in March I thought I'd felt nervous at football, but that was nothing compared to the away game at Oldham. The day started well enough. I set off from Derby on a sunny spring morning and had a hassle free trip up north. I was on my own as one of my usual travelling companions was working and the other was at a wedding.

After finding the ground it was a just a quick walk to the The Rifle Range. Some of the PISA regulars were already there. We listened to Andy Mills' tales from the Free Kicks Foundation's '92 Grounds In 92 Hours'. Andy had been ill during the trip and in the photos he looks like the corpse from Weekend At Bernie's. On arrival at the ground I put up a couple of the smaller flags. It didn't look as though there was going to be room for the PISA flag. The away end was filling quickly, and even after I'd been in my seat for a while people were still streaming in.

Posh started the match brightly and Aaron McLean could have had us an early lead but he shot wide. The news came through that Millwall had taken the lead but moments later our nerves were calmed by a goal from Mackail-Smith. Coutts' cross had rebounded off Boyd's chest and Mackail-Smith scuffed in the shot. Cue jubilation amongst the away fans and a torrent of abuse from the very angry looking children immediately to our right. News of a Walsall equaliser at Millwall was also well received.

Oldham finished the half stronger. A poor Lewis punch from a corner went unpunished when Dean Keates cleared off the line, but their equaliser came from another set piece. Chris Taylor found himself unmarked from a free kick and he made no mistake. Worse was to follow. Just moments later Taylor picked up the ball in midfield and played a through ball to Alessanda whose shot from the edge of the box beat Lewis. His celebrations were short lived though. The referee had ruled the goal out. We weren't quite sure why. The linesman hadn't flagged for anything, although that didn't stop a couple of guys from Oldham's main stand running half the length of the pitch to berate him. Watching a replay later showed that the striker had pulled back Tom Williams and the ref had made a very good decision. Having just got to half-time level we checked other scores and found Millwall and MK both leading. News of Leicester losing had already filtered through.

The second-half was a quieter affair both on the pitch and in the stands. I think most people were so nervous that with those below us winning and Leicester having equalised, dropping points would really hurt us. With about five mins to go and Posh looking unlikely to get a winner, a hopeful punt forward caught out Oldham's keeper and centre back under pressure from Mackail-Smith. The centre back nudged the ball past the onrushing keeper leaving Mackail-Smith the simple task of walking the ball into the net. That was the cue for wild celebrations in the Posh end and for many of the Oldham fans to head for the exit. After four excruciating mins of injury time the ref finally blew for full time leaving fans and players alike to celebrate another hard fought win. I felt emotionally drained after the game. Later we discovered Leicester had scored at about the same time as us, unlike us though they had conceded an equaliser deep into injury time. The gap at the top was now down to two points and the race for the title was well and truly on.

*Keith Gilmour*

A few seasons back Peterborough United couldn't string three passes together. In a year which one way or another became the end of an era, a Sky mockumentary was allowed behind the scenes to observe a collection of has-beens and petulant wannabees create a new disaster movie. As a Poshie it could make you cry. For the second time the club was subject to national TV ridicule. Sometimes, when the house is quiet and it's dark outside, I can still hear the sound of Sean St Ledger's studs hitting the dressing room floor.

Roll forward to Boundary Park and the contrast couldn't be greater as nearly a thousand Posh fans watched Posh make it a seventh win in a row and put us a mere two points behind leaders Leicester.

We drove up on the Saturday morning to Radcliffe where my mate Ben lives. Benno is an exiled Poshie but being in Manchester has meant that over the last two seasons we have had the choice of seeing games at Morecombe, Accrington, Bury, Leeds, Oldham and Stockport. We made it to the ground a good 40 mins before kick-off, where everyone was relieved that, for once, I had purchased the correct number of tickets!

In a game that could largely be described as forgettable (I have forgotten it), there was little that stood out apart from the stark warning provided by the state of Oldham's ground. It is hard to believe that Oldham were ever in the top division. Those who moan about London Road would do well to visit places like Boundary Park and Barnet's shed at Underhill, but these are the grounds that make lower league football and give it the character that may be in short supply when we visit Premiership stadia on a weekly basis. I will miss the 1930s toilets, the terracing, the scaffold media centres, wooden seats and inaudible tannoy announcements. However I will not miss grounds that are so one dimensional, the vocal home support decides to plonk itself next to the away end, thus creating a miners strike atmosphere with the Thin Fluorescent Line deployed between the two. Oldham was like a trip back into the '80s, minus the seat throwing. The desperation of a club on the edge of the play-offs was evident in the behaviour of its supporters. One was so incensed at a linesman's decision he propelled himself down from the stand, his straggly hair, faded brown leather jacket and oversized jeans making for a comedy image as he screamed angrily at the indifferent official.

Posh once again showed the form of champions. Oldham was a hard fought victory led by Mackail-Smith, whose persistence and energy was rewarded with two goals. Williams and Zakuani went off injured in the closing battles and for the last ten minutes the Posh defence was down to the proverbial 'bare bones'. Fortunately for Ferguson the belief he has shown in the squad by not frittering away DMac's money in the transfer window was rewarded again and again as players who had been out of the limelight, seasoned pro Chris Westwood and injury plagued Shane Blackett, stepped up when it mattered.

Wherever we are in seven years, these are the seasons that will give us memories like those that my father's generation have of the great Midland League team that took us into the league in the 1960s. The names of the players and management team that we see now are the ones we will remember in the future, players whose will to succeed and not just pick up a pay cheque have dragged the club up from the depths of TV despair and given us back our stolen pride.

*Steve Turner*

**10/04/09**

## Peterborough United 1 - 1 Cheltenham Town

McLean '36 Hutton '66

Att: 9,817 (212 away).

**Peterborough United:** Joe Lewis, Russell Martin, Shane Blackett, Chris Westwood, Charlie Lee, Aaron McLean, George Boyd, Dean Keates, Craig Mackail-Smith, Paul Coutts, Shaun Batt (-78')
Subs: James McKeown, Sergio Torres, Billy Crook, Dominic Green (+78'), Danny Blanchett
**Cheltenham Town:** Scott Brown, Shane Duff, Michael Townsend, John Finnigan (-46'), Paul Connor, Andy Lindegaard (-78'), Andy Gallinagh, Drissa Diallo, Frankie Artus (-62'), Michail Antonio, Yuri Berchiche
Subs: Dave Bird (+46'), Will Puddy, Kyle Haynes, Leon Constantine (+78'), David Hutton (+62')

7.30am: Knock on the door and the bloke next door wants to cut his lawn early as it's going to rain: "no problem mate I'll do mine at 11-30pm tonight"

7.35: Chug, chug, chuuuuuuuugggggggggg that's the sound of a mower that's not been serviced since Sept 2008

7.40: Off for my run

7.45: Did OK on my run up for a shower

8.00: Weetabix and orange juice for breakfast followed but last night's takeaway from the fridge

8.30: Back to bed, wife calling

8.33: Up and thinking of Chelt at home

9.00: Cut my lawn LOL

10.00: Phone call from a client that lasted two hours.

12.00 Another shower (I'm a clean bloke you see)

1.30: Arrive at Ebs

2-00: The ale is flowing, old faces in abundance, nice chat with Dr Cyclops about the 70s etc and an even better one with Mitch about this book.

2.30: Time to make a move

2.50: LRE shut, run like hell for the Moy's, well err actually walked like hell.

3.05: Met some old Posh.netters in the queue which went from a nice queue to a scramble at 3.15 when the shout went up that the Moy's was full.

3.26: I got in and good to be in the Moy's again, (wink, wink) nice atmosphere, went down for a fag and 30 secs later the stadium erupts. 1-0 Posh

4.00: Met up with a couple of 70s lads for the second half and I'll be buggered if we didn't miss the equalizer. Those around us reckon Lewis messed up big time.

4.45: Left the stadium, feeling pissed off we'd again succumbed to big game nerves. Roll on Millwall away.

*Paul Donnelly*

* * * * *

**13/04/09**

## Millwall 2 - 0 Peterborough United

Martin '25 (pen)
Price '58

Att: 10,518 (899 away).

**Millwall:** David Forde, Zak Whitbread, Gary Alexander, Richard Duffy (-74'), Tony Craig, Scott Barron, Dave Martin, Marc Laird, Nadjim Abdou, Jason Price, Adam Bolder
Subs: Neil Harris, Lewis Grabban, Chris Hackett, Ali Fuseini (+74'), Lenny Pidgeley
**Peterborough United:** Joe Lewis, Russell Martin, Shane Blackett (-46'), Charlie Lee, Aaron McLean, George Boyd (-79'), Dean Keates, Craig Mackail-Smith, Paul Coutts, Chris Whelpdale (-61'), Gabriel Zakuani
Subs: Chris Westwood (+46'), James McKeown, Sergio Torres, Shaun Batt (+61'), Dominic Green (+79')

Our day started early at 8.30am after leaving the car at Cockfosters we were off for a sightseeing day in fancy London, which included travelling on a World War 2 Duck Tour around London by road and water, a walk along South Bank where we took in a bit of culture at the Globe Theatre and then made our way to the Clink Prison to see methods of imprisonment and torture from years gone by.

After a nice dinner at a pub at Euston we made our way to the New Den ready for a warm South London welcome. We had already heard that Leicester had beaten Dirty Leeds and the Imposters had beaten Bristol Rovers which meant that the game was even more important.

Transport for London had decided to do work on the underground, so it was off the train at New Cross Gate and walking down to the ground. We followed the signs to the ground which took us through some dodgy housing estates mixing with Millwall fans and gobby chavs. On my mum and dad's instructions I was the quietest I'd been all day. We arrived at the ground and my mum said she had never been so pleased to see fellow Posh fans.

Once in the ground I stripped off and donned my beloved Posh shirt and then a chap from Millwall came and asked if I wanted to be a mascot. My dad and I made our way down to the pitch. At first he was going to take us under the stand in our Posh shirts when the stewards panicked and said to take us around the pitch which was good because I would have been crapping my pants.

Whilst waiting to lead out the team I suddenly thought, 'I'm going to be on Sky Sports'. I'd chosen to walk out with Boydy! The noise of the crowd was loud but I could hear the Posh fans singing. After standing in the line up I ran around a bit not really knowing what to do. Then it was kick off and back to our seats. If the roar of their fans was meant to be intimidating, it wasn't as we were making just as much noise.

Not a lot of Posh pressure except a header over the bar by McLean and a free kick by Keates, then that penalty. I have never heard so much noise or seen my dad so angry at what was going on. Every Posh fan in the ground must have gone through every emotion in those few minutes, dread, elation ,disbelief, then anger. After that I sang my heart out willing the team on. 1-0 to the referee was a favourite, along with Posh are going up, going up, Posh are going up. But the one that stayed in my mind 2-0 down who gives a f*** , we're super Posh and we're going up.

The end of the game saw me hiding my Posh shirt again as we made our way back to the train via a safer route. On arriving at London Bridge station Millwall chavs were chanting 'Waaaaaaaaallllll. Mum said that's what you get when you let children drink!

The next day saw us going to Wembley stadium for a tour, and whilst walking down Wembley way I was thinking please God don't let me be here in five weeks time.

*Ashley Thorpe*

* * * * *

**18/04/09**

## Peterborough United 1 - 0 Stockport County

Mackail-Smith '25

Att: 8,333 (284 away).

**Peterborough United:** Joe Lewis, Russell Martin, Craig Morgan, Chris Westwood, Charlie Lee, Aaron McLean, George Boyd, Dean Keates, Craig Mackail-Smith, Paul Coutts (-87'), Dominic Green (-59')
Subs: Lee Frecklington (+87'), James McKeown, Chris Whelpdale (+59'), Shaun Batt, Danny Blanchett
**Stockport County:** Conrad Logan, Chris O'Grady (-74'), Peter Thompson, Tommy Rowe, Michael Raynes, Paul Turnbull, Leon McSweeney, Greg Tansey (-46'), Josh Thompson, James Vincent, Andy Halls (-33')
Subs: Michael Rose, Daniel Rowe (+46'), Matty Mainwaring (+74'), Oli Johnson (+33'), Craig Roberts

Tense, comfortable, frustrating, dominant, edgy, at times gloriously fluid; watching Posh today was to see a snapshot of the last few months' charge towards promotion. A sumptuous first half performance should have seen us out of sight by half-time but Green hit the post when an open goal beckoned and the nerves of the crowd seemed to transmit to the players. Only the post - left quivering after a close-range Johnson piledriver - denied Stockport a point. Posh deserved the win but struggled to deliver the final blow against a poor Stockport team and the heightened expectations of 8,000 tense fans.

*Harry Sunford*

*"Promotion is getting closer by the game and we can taste it now. This was obviously a crucial win, but I was particularly impressed by the way we achieved it. It was only 1-0 in the end, but we were worthy winners. Some of the football the lads produced in the first half was outstanding considering the pressure of the occasion."*

*Darren Ferguson*

* * * * *

**24/04/09**

*"I've had a feeling for a while that it will go right down to the wire and I haven't changed my mind. We are fully focused on our own game tomorrow. We know we need to win and we know that it won't be easy as Colchester are a very good side with a very good manager. But the lads have been sharp in training and they look in the mood to give a good performance and get another three points. We will have to be at our best to win though."*

*Darren Ferguson*

* * * * *

**25/04/09**

## Colchester United 0-1 Peterborough United
Lee '40

Att: 6,532.

**Colchester United:** Dean Gerken, John White, Matt Lockwood, Chris Coyne, Clive Platt, Kem ?zzet, Mark Yeates, Pat Baldwin, Ashley Vincent (-77'), Simon Hackney (-70'), Marc Tierney
Subs: Matt Heath (+77'), Mark Cousins, Anthony Wordsworth (+70'), Sam Corcoran
**Peterborough United:** Joe Lewis, Russell Martin, Craig Morgan, Charlie Lee, Aaron McLean (-89'), George Boyd, Dean Keates (-60'), Craig Mackail-Smith, Paul Coutts, Chris Whelpdale, Gabriel Zakuani
Subs: Chris Westwood, Lee Frecklington (+60'), James McKeown, Shaun Batt (+89'), Dominic Green

Consider the hourglass. I did, as I sat outside Mortimer station (a rural halt south of Reading) waiting for Webby. Does the sand in an hourglass flow constantly from one bulb to the other, or does the weight of sand increase the flow-rate when it's first flipped over? When was the last time you even set eyes on an hourglass? Every day is the surprising answer if you use a PC. Microsoft uses one to mark the eternity that passes when loading programmes or files.

This was, of course, a diversionary tactic. Having spent all night tossing and turning and trying not to think about today's match I had at last found something to occupy my mind. A set of South West carriages slid silently into Platform One bound for Reading, wrong train. I wondered about the Posh fans in the City, and elsewhere, who were heading for Colchester. What was their state of mind right now and were they dog-tired like me? All thoughts of tiredness were banished as soon as we set off. We quickly agreed that promotion really ought to be secured as soon as possible and if that meant missing the moment because it happened in Northampton, so be it. How little we knew.

It's a stroke of genius to direct fans into a town-centre station car park then bus them all out again to a venue. The buses ran smoothly and the journey was just quick enough so there was no time to pass-out from the peculiar smell. The snappily titled WHCS was far easier on the eye than I'd imagined though the barcode-reading automated turnstiles utterly defeated many Posh fans. For them no amount of random prodding of tickets into slots, pushing against turnstiles or pressing light bulbs would let them through.

Even 90 minutes before kick-off the concourse was packed. Although Colchester had sneakily priced the beer and lager at £3.10 (for 500 ml), it deterred no one, though fans did struggle comically to hold a drink and fiddle with ill-fitting fancy dress at the same time. My seat was R5. R for 'right at the back' and the 5 seat from the side wall, nice. The steep rake of the stand made for a brisk climb and if I'd got a penny for every time a Posh fan moaned about the lack of handrail, lift or escalator, I'd have made £1.32. By kick-off the stand was packed. I couldn't see an empty seat, aside from the thousands elsewhere in the stadium of course. The Posh fans in home areas were doing an excellent job of hiding at this stage.

I've never been one to write detailed match reports because I usually end up going a bit Chris Kamara with my descriptions, but it's probably worth mentioning one or two highlights from this historic encounter. Lynford

Christie always talked about starting a race 'on the B of the Bang.' Charlie Lee must be a 'Lunchbox' fan. His second minute run from the halfway line into the box had all of us on our feet in anticipation. There's an amusing trend for squad players to adopt similar hairstyles and most of Colchester's team sported shaved heads - probably expecting their appearance to intimidate opponents. George Boyd wasn't in the mood to be intimidated. He isn't flash and he probably couldn't execute a Cruyff turn if his life depended on it, but somehow he hypnotises defenders and glides serenely through flailing legs like a butterfly through a summer meadow. If that sounds a bit flowery, well, that's just how it is with George.

Charlie's goal was a belter, literally. He said in an interview afterwards that, having missed his chance so early in the game, he was always going to put his foot through the ball next time. And it was George, floating past yet another clumsy challenge, who set him up. Our stand erupted. A goal is good at any time, but scoring just before the break creates a buzz on the concourse as well as in the dressing room. Colchester's only real chance of the half was a free kick just outside the box. No sooner had my heart started to pound when I glanced over at Joe's positioning and realised the kick would have to nestle in the top corner of the near post to beat the lad. It didn't.

Thousands of pre-match pints have to go somewhere at half-time. The queue for the urinal trough was five-deep in most places and a plaintive cry to "get a move on" was met with one bloke shouting back "I can't piss with people looking." The stadium architect had massively under-specified the toilet furniture too, and two sinks with one hand dryer forced many to abandon their personal hygiene routine. Back in my seat a quick glance on the BBC mobile website revealed 0-0 at Stadium:MK, all good so far.

Posh rarely give what pundits like to call 'a 90-minute performance', meaning that at some stage during every game there's a period where players and their concentration levels meander aimlessly like a bloke waiting for his partner in a clothes shop. There were no such let-ups today and I was thoroughly impressed with the collective team effort when Colchester had possession. The tackling was the tough side of legal with defenders and midfielders throwing themselves around to prevent key passes or shots at goal. I honestly don't remember Joe making a save in the second half.

Frecklington, sponsored by NHS Direct, replaced the limping Keates but there was no discernable drop in tempo. George continued to embarrass his markers and even managed a lung-busting (for him) run down the left wing before sending over an inch-perfect cross for CMS. Shame that Gerken was flinging himself towards the home sponsor's man of the match award.

Then came a moment that the 2,000 Posh fans present will never ever forget. Someone, somewhere on the left hand side of the stand was either listening to a radio or received a text message. His cheer may have been involuntary, but the cheer instantly became a roar that travelled at warp speed along the fans and, in the blink of an eye, everyone was celebrating madly. "Walsall must've scored" said a particularly astute Posh fan. I muttered an expletive, were we really going to be promoted today?

The racket must have affected the players and, obviously, they would know the cause but the match simply continued as before; Posh dominating, Gerken saving, Colchester making no progress with their meagre possession. I suddenly started thinking about the hourglass again. I just couldn't get the image out of my head. This match, the match at Stadium:MK and our progress towards promotion were being played out with a smooth, inevitable effluxion of time. In similar circumstances with such intense pressure I would normally be passing enough bricks to build a small detached house but now I was completely calm.

I confess I winced at Tierney's blistering shot in the middle of the four minutes of stoppage time and only Joe knows if the ball whistled as loudly as it appeared from 120 yards away. Then it was all over. I can't possibly claim to know why everyone else was so elated, for me it was the joy that we'd won the last remaining tough fixture and a huge burden was lifted. I was still so calm I was ready to accept news of a late equaliser elsewhere.

There were no public announcements to tell us what was happening and the large screen stubbornly displayed an advert for a poxy local company that will probably go bust in the recession, but everyone was smiling. The players made their way towards us and we all celebrated a job well done - but still no news. The Sky TV camera, high up to our left, focussed on Fergie while we belted out a never-ending rendition of We are Going Up. Then the manager ran forward and jumped on Joe's back and we all went completely and utterly mental.

Seat R5 was a long way from where the players were singing, dancing and embracing each other in front of the fans, but I didn't mind. With the initial euphoria behind me I could now feel tears welling up in my eyes. It had been almost 17 years since I last felt like this. My throat felt raw from the singing. I clapped and sang along with everyone else and I watched. I watched the biggest smiles in the world on the faces of elderly Posh fans. I watched other fans hugging as they jumped up and down. I even watched some of the remaining Colchester fans as they watched us and noted their smiles; uninhibited joy is wonderfully infectious.

A day later and a YouTube clip of the final minutes on Sky's Soccer Saturday revealed how grossly premature all our celebrations had been. Fergie was misinformed by a BBC reporter who was taking his newsfeed from Auntie's Final Score programme, it had called 'time' at Stadium:MK when in fact the match was being held up by a serious injury. When Sky's John Salako eventually confirmed the final whistle, Jeff Stelling back in the studio announced that Posh could now start their party… he was way too late. The clip made me think again of the first Posh fan to celebrate Walsall's goal. At the time he must have felt like Lieutenant Lapenotiere, the naval officer who took news of Nelson's victory at Trafalgar back to London. I wondered what that Posh fan felt like as he waited to hear that Walsall had beaten MK, what a day he had.

Outside the ground again and there were small groups of Colchester supporters with charity collection buckets. I emptied both pockets of change and they were delighted (there was at least £1.32). I told them it was a great time to be collecting and they wished me well. The Us fans waiting for buses back to town shook hands and patted backs enthusiastically. The sun shone and we went home very, very happy.

*Phil Keys*

The fans are like a good woman. Always there when you need them - feasting on the success and then quick to nag when things go wrong. But true love, happiness and the potential to be given an occasional orgasm - like today - leaves a smile on their face and keeps them loyal forever.

*Nigel Curtis*

## MK Dons 0-1 Walsall

Ibehre 61

* * * * *

**30/04/09**

| | | P | W | D | L | Pts |
|---|---|---|---|---|---|---|
| 1 | Leicester | 45 | 26 | 15 | 4 | 93 |
| 2 | Posh | 45 | 26 | 10 | 9 | 88 |
| 3 | MK Dons | 45 | 25 | 9 | 11 | 84 |

# May

"Wrong f*****g door" shouted Adi, as I buffooned my way into Ebeneezer's – a sort of working man's social club type effort where Peterborough fans congregate to drink and then drink a bit more and then fall over or argue or just drink a little bit more. Like a confused old sod, I'm often overwhelmed by new scenarios. I never know where to put myself or who to say what to, and the initial 'entering' is usually an immensely traumatic part of my night. I hate 'entering'. And entering Ebeneezer's, with its glittery purple backdropped stage and chairs of a thousand stains, was confusingly not what I expected.

This season I decided to make an internet TV series for ITV, and write a book about my adventures as the ultimate gloryhunter - picking a team randomly, supporting them until they lose and then supporting the team who beat them. All season. And, for good measure, going to live in the place as well.

So imagine what this season has been like for a social retard like me: basically, a whole load of 'entering'. I've wandered alien parts of the country for 10 months in a spinny daze, sometimes not knowing what end of the country I was waking up in. And I wasn't just entering a new pub or bar, but the home ends of clubs I don't congenitally support. Gulp.

There I was, bumbling around, self-consciously, always with a conspicuous camera on a stick that somehow always made me feel grubby, like I was trying to film things just out of decency's reach. Maybe sometimes I was. And often a lot of the fans knew that the bloke with the moody camera on a stick, who they've seen gurning in the local paper this week…is a Spurs fan.

At the start and probably each time I moved clubs, I had visions of coins, pies, big-knuckled tattoed fists smothered in ropey old gold smacking my mooey. But it didn't end up like that. Fans at a lot of clubs accepted my Spurs-shaped hand of friendship. Not least at Peterborough. Adi Mowles, the leader of Peterborough's Independent Supporters Association, affects an endearing harshness - unless discussing Mr. Fry - and I knew as soon as I got that first Kronenburg down my neck, I'd wandered in amongst a warm-spirited, close-knit bunch who care about their club and those associated with it.

As an outsider I would say it generally takes, on average, three games with the fans of another club before that creeping fondness, that little bit of give-a-monkeys about whether they win or lose begins to emerge. My first game with Posh, at home to Scunthorpe, saw give-a-damn emerge around half way through the second period, when the best football I'd seen all year blunderbusted me among the home crowd – including Adi and his slight resemblance to the lion from Wizard of Oz – going mental-ballistic in the London Road enclosure. Saliva up the walls, forbidden embraces with the bloke next to you (who you've never spoken to) and contorted faces so twisted with pleasure that they bore no resemblance to the owner. That night was one of my most memorable - not only at Posh, but across the entire season.

Just like I did at places like Brentford and Darlo, I went on to meet a bizarre menagerie of characters around the club. Where else do you see people so different, drawn together to support the same cause? There was Howard, the Fabio Capello lookalike, there was Mr Posh himself (Mick), there was another bloke who seemed to genuinely want to marry George Boyd and there was the bunch who raced around 92 league grounds in 92 hours for charity. Not to mention the other deeply pleasant oddities I encountered at all the games I went to. Especially not to mention what I saw one night on that purple sparkly stage at Eboneezer's. Good grief.

I genuinely thought I might end my season amid the glory of promotion with Posh, but then entered Millwall, followed by Bristol Rovers and just weeks later I ended up on the last day of the season with the merest of glories – surviving relegation with Brighton. I suppose that's all a gloryhunter deserves. This journey, on the face of it, was about chasing glory at whatever cost. But really, it wasn't. It was a guided tour around the devoted fans who support their local team and stick with them through thick and thin. That's what this game's all about.

Glory is relative. And this season, it was relatively special down at Posh.

*Spencer Austin,*
*The Gloryhunter*

Unlike the other submissions to this book, I have not attended a game this season. In fact, I have not seen the 'Mac Attack', the 'White Pele' or 'Teflon Joe' as I have not made it home from the USA during the season.

After following the Posh since 1970, these past two seasons have been the only ones where I have not seen at least one game. And as the guy that turned around and went home to London when I was half way to the famous 'Best Posh Game of all Time' at Huddersfield in 92 I'm seriously beginning to doubt my judgment.

So, these past two seasons I actually haven't missed a game – via the Posh World subscription coverage to uncle Edwin's commentary and Bob Burrows bellowing "AND THE POSH ARE ON THE ATTACK – PENALTY" every 10 minutes.

Most Saturday's begin for me with a cup of coffee at 6.30am and the opening up of three windows on my laptop : www.theposh.com (for the commentary), www.londonroad.net (for the banter) and www.sportinglife.com (for the live scores and live tables.) By 9.00am my wife and kids normally know how well we've played as they have heard me roar at every Posh goal (the cats tend to run and hide under the sofa) or remain silent when we lose. Of course, nothing beats being there at the game but following Posh via the web is so much better than when I moved to the USA in 1993. When the londonroad.net site was launched, I would type updates to the Posh messageboard as Mick Bratley phoned me after each goal.

However, two games stand out for me this season for very different reasons. On 7 March I was in Shanghai, jetlagged and unable to sleep. I didn't think that I would be able to stay awake for the 11.00pm (local time) kick off for Hartlepool away but by the time Porter had hit the underside of the bar in the last minute, I was on the edge of my seat, raiding the mini-bar for alcoholic help and unable to go to sleep for another 2 hours.

Fast forward five weeks and it's Monday 13 April. I'm flying to Ottawa via Toronto and have a 90 minute lay-over between flights. I do what every ex-pat Poshie does and log onto JustinTV to watch the second half of Millwall v Posh. As I logged on, I knew we were 1-0 down but did not know of the thrice taken penalty fiasco. I then watch Posh get outworked, outplayed and outfought for 45 minutes wondering what I have done to deserve this. It's the first time I get to see George Boyd and he is well shackled by the Millwall defense. I almost miss the flight to Ottawa as I stare in disbelief at the e-mails from Millwall supporting friends telling me that we're going to bottle it.

Getting promoted is a big deal for the ex-pats – we will get to see the Posh on TV or via the computer much more regularly than has been the norm - hopefully, they'll put on a show or two for the cameras.

*Paul Miller*

* * * * *

02/05/09

## Peterborough United 2 - 2 Swindon Town

Mackail-Smith '40 Cox '17
Keates '90 Cox '42

Att: 10,886 (863 away).

**Peterborough United:** Joe Lewis (-77'), Russell Martin,Craig Morgan, Charlie Lee, Aaron McLean, George Boyd, Dean Keates, Craig Mackail-Smith Goal (-71'), Paul Coutts, Dominic Green (-77'),Gabriel Zakuani
Subs: Chris Westwood, Lee Frecklington (+71'), James McKeown (+77'), Sergio Torres, Shaun Batt (+77')
**Swindon Town:** Phil Smith, Jamie Vincent, Michael Timlin, Jerel Ifil, Craig Easton (-77'), Jon-Paul McGovern, Lilian Nalis (-60'), Billy Paynter, Jean-François Lescinel, Simon Cox (-89'), Owain Tudur-Jones
Subs: Jack Smith, Anthony McNamee (+89'), Kevin Amankwah (+60'), Mark Marshall (+77'), Hamdi Razak

I was standing in Sydney airport on Friday afternoon waiting to check in and thinking that this must be the craziest thing I have ever done and definitely the furthest I have travelled for the love of Posh. It's even more mental than driving to Wigan on a Tuesday night, in the middle of a fuel crisis, to watch them play. There was no way, however, that I could miss the greatest achievement that Posh have accomplished for 15 years.

After having decided that I wanted to go the final game of the season on the Monday, I was so terrified that I wouldn't be able to get a ticket to the sold out game. I had booked my flight already and hoped that it would not be in vain. Luckily one of the regular posters on posh.net came through for me and the ticket was in the post by Tuesday.

So it was up and away and 23 hours and a train ride later I was sitting in Ebs, surrounded by people in Posh shirts with a pint in one hand and a Red Bull in the other, enjoying talking about the expectations and speculations of next season. There was a sense of relief that Posh had spared us a nail biting last game by achieving promotion a game early.

London Road was packed with around 10,000 Posh fans who were creating a great atmosphere. It was party time. The outcome of the game was going to be irrelevant so it was just a case of sitting back, relaxing and enjoying the football. Posh went behind twice in the first half despite creating quite a few chances although I have to confess that I did miss CMS's goal due to a quick toilet break. Don't you just hate it when that happens? The game finished 2-2 after the second half saw McLean miss a penalty before Keates finally equalised with a screamer of a free kick.

Now it was the players turn to join the party with the receipt of their promotion medals. It took a long time to get here, for both myself and Posh, and I wouldn't have missed it for the world. Bring on the Newcastle!

*Vicky Harrison*

So, for the second successive season 10,000 fans, including my dad, my son and myself, trundle down to London Road to watch a Peterborough United promotion party. Who would have thought it when only three years ago we were a fourth division club going nowhere and stars of our very own sitcom on Sky TV?

Walking down London Road past the hoards of street sellers only seen before at the likes of premiership and international football grounds. Flags of all sizes, t-shirts of various designs and pie sellers with clean aprons; this is the MacAnthony dream in full swing.

We decide to go into the ground early to soak up the atmosphere and pay for a new centre forward by purchasing two beers and a hot dog. Then to our seats. A carnival atmosphere was already in full swing with giant inflatable 'things' on the pitch, a band playing and kids waving their newly purchased flags and annoying every adult within poking distance.

The ground soon filled and it seemed such a shame that Moy's End was not given to Posh fans and the few hundred Swindon fans accommodated in the seats. Still, a nice touch from Swindon as they made a 'tunnel' for the Posh players who were met with a roar and standing ovation from the faithful and the other three thousand new fans.

And to the game. Much like the Darlington match twelve months' earlier it didn't seem to matter what was happening on the pitch and the players seemed to think likewise. A dreadful ball across the backline from newly crowned Player of the Season (six times I think) Charlie Lee and the much coveted Swindon forward Simon Cox gratefully put the visitors ahead. This stirred Posh into action and George Boyd was soon all over the pitch taking on the Swindon backline on his own. One fine run down the right and he swept the ball across, top scorer Craig Mackail Smith got in front of his defender and put the ball home. 10,000 rose to their feet and all found their voice in unison. However, Swindon refused to read the plot and that man Cox pounced on another error at the back to make it 2-1 at half time.

Scenes below the stand gave a hint of what must lay in store in the Championship. Queues for everything from relieving oneself to relieving ones wallet. The only downside at this continued success at Posh seems to be a very ageing ground just not able to cope with large gates.

Onto the second half and Posh come out to put on a display. Boyd continued to embarrass any defender who dare come near him and soon he makes an unbelievable run beating three or four players in his stride only to be upended by a Swindon defender in the box. The ref waves play on determined not to miss out in front of a large crowd and then makes amends by giving a penalty moments later for a nothing challenge on Boyd. Aaron McLean gives their keeper a bit of shot stopping practise and we seem to be heading for defeat in our final game once more. One cleared off the line and two fine stops by their keeper and it looks all over until we win a free kick on the edge of the area. Two minutes into stoppage time and unsung hero Dean Keates steps forward and sends a delightful free kick right into the corner leaving the Swindon keeper with no chance. Again 10,000 go wild and the promotion party is back in full swing.

Another unbelievable season since chairman Darragh MacAnthony rode into town. Where will this all end? Is the Premiership really within reach? Stuff that dreams are made of for a little football club which has languished in the lower divisions for far too long. So many highlights and for me this season has topped the last. We've beaten so-called big clubs in Leeds and Leicester, played some unbelievably attractive football, scored some memorable goals and thoroughly deserved automatic promotion for the second season running.

Well done Darren Ferguson, well done Darragh MacAnthony, well done the players and staff but most of all, well done to all the fans. A lot of us have stuck by this club through thick and thin with a hell of an emphasis on the thin. These are the type of days that have kept us going all these years. We are at last living the dream and long may it continue.

*Gary Miller*

And the Cobblers were relegated. What a perfect season.

* * * * *

02/05/09

| | | P | W | D | L | Pts |
|---|---|---|---|---|---|---|
| 1 | Leicester | 46 | 27 | 15 | 4 | 96 |
| 2 | Posh | 46 | 26 | 11 | 9 | 89 |
| 3 | MK Dons | 46 | 26 | 9 | 11 | 87 |